THE SCOTTISH CLANS
AND THEIR TARTANS

FORTY-SEVENTH PRINTING

HISTORY OF EACH CLAN AND
FULL LIST OF SEPTS

CASSELL LTD.

CASSELL LTD.
1 Vincent Square, London SW1P 2PN

First Published about 1891
Forty-seventh printing 1985

British Library Cataloguing in Publication Data

The Scottish clans and their tartans.
  1. Tartans
  929'.2'09411   DA880.H76

  ISBN 0-304-31114-6

Printed and bound in Spain by,
Artes Gráficas Grijelmo SA, Bilbao

CONTENTS

	PAGE
THE LANGUAGE OF THE GAEL	7
THE HIGHLAND DRESS AND HOW TO WEAR IT	9
WOMEN'S HIGHLAND DRESS	12
CLAN CEREMONIAL	13
GAELIC PERSONAL NAMES AND SURNAMES	15
FEMALE PERSONAL NAMES	21
CHIEFSHIP AND CHIEFTAINCY	22
ARMORIAL BEARINGS	23
DESIGNATIONS OF HIGHLAND CHIEFS AND FAMILIES	24
A LIST OF CLAN SEPTS AND DEPENDENTS	28
WHAT TARTAN CAN I WEAR?	50
THE SCOTTISH CLAN SYSTEM	51
CLAN MAP OF SCOTLAND	54

Clans in Alphabetical Order with Plates Photographed from Actual Tartans

Clan	Plate	Clan	Plate
Anderson	1	Lamont	33
Brodie of Brodie	2	Leslie	34
The House of Bruce	3	Lindsay	35
Buchanan	4	MacAlister	36
Cameron	5	MacAlpine	37
Cameron of Lochiel	6	MacArthur	38
Campbell of Argyll	7	MacAulay	39
Campbell of		MacCallum or Malcolm	40
Breadalbane	8	MacDonald	41
Chisholm	9	MacDonald of	
Colquhoun	10	Clanranald	42
Cumming	11	MacDonald of Sleat	43
Davidson	12	MacDonell of Glengarry	44
Douglas	13	MacDonell of Keppoch	45
Drummond	14	MacDougall	46
Erskine	15	MacDuff and Duff	47
Farquharson	16	MacEwen	48
Fergusson	17	MacFarlane	49
Forbes	18	Macfie or MacPhee	50
Forty-Second Royal		MacGillivray	51
Highland Regiment		MacGregor	52
(The Black Watch)	19	Macinnes (Clan	
Fraser	20	Aonghais)	53
Gordon	21	Macintyre	54
Gow and MacGowan	22	Mackay	55
Graham	23	MacKenzie	56
Grant	24	Mackinlay	57
Gunn	25	Mackinnon	58
Hamilton	26	Mackintosh	59
Hay	27	MacLachlan	60
Henderson (Mac-		Maclaine of Lochbuie	61
Kendricks)	28	MacLaren	62
Innes	29	MacLean	63
Johnston	30	Maclennan	64
Kennedy	31	Macleod of Macleod	65
Kerr	32	MacLeod of Lewis	66

Clan	Plate	Clan	Plate
Macmillan	67	Robertson (Clann	
Macnab	68	Donnachaidh)	83
MacNaughten	69	Rose	84
MacNeil of Barra	70	Ross	85
McNeill of Colonsay	71	Scott	86
Macpherson	72	Sinclair	87
Macquarrie	73	Skene	88
Macqueen	74	Royal Stewart	89
Macrae	75	Dress Stewart	90
Matheson	76	Hunting Stewart	91
Maxwell	77	Stewart of Appin	92
Menzies	78	Stewart of Atholl	93
Morrison	79	Sutherland	94
Munro	80	Urquhart	95
Murray of Atholl	81	Wallace	96
Ogilvy	82		

The publishers would like to acknowledge with thanks the help of the following : Kinloch Anderson, Esq., of Anderson's Edinburgh ; the National Museum of Antiquities of Scotland, Edinburgh.

THE LANGUAGE OF THE GAEL

THE native tongue of the Gael is called Gaelic. The Gaelic of Ireland, Scotland and the Isle of Man are closely connected ; indeed, till the Reformation, and for a century or more thereafter, the Irish and Scottish Gaelic had a common literary language, though the spoken tongues had diverged considerably. In the eighteenth century Scottish Gaelic broke away completely from the Irish and began a literary career of its own with a literary dialect that could be understood easily all over the Highlands and Islands. Manx is more allied to the Scottish Gaelic than it is to the Irish ; it is generally understood to be a remnant of the Gaelic of the Kingdom of the Isles.

Irish Gaelic is the dialect of the greatest number of Gaels, and contains almost all the old literature. It is divided into the following four leading periods :

I. OLD IRISH (O.Ir.), from about A.D. 800 to 1000. Besides some scraps of poetry and prose, we have *The Book of Armagh* (tenth century), which contains continuous Old Irish narrative.

II. EARLY IRISH (E.Ir.), from A.D. 1000 to 1200. The two great MSS. of " *Lebor na h-uidre* "—*The Book of the Dun Cow* and *The Book of Leinster*—mark this period.

III. MIDDLE IRISH (M.Ir.), from A.D. 1200 to about 1550. The chief MSS. are *The Yellow Book of Lecan*, *The Book of Ballimote*, and the " *Leabar Breac* " or *Speckled Book*, and *The Book of Lismore*.

IV. MODERN or NEW IRISH, here called Irish (Ir.), from 1550 to the present time.

The literary language of Ireland and Scotland remained the same till about 1700. The oldest document of Scottish Gaelic is *The Book of Deer*, a MS. which contains half a dozen entries in Gaelic of grants of land made to the monastery of Deer. " The

entries," says the late Dr. MacBain, " belong to the eleventh
and twelfth centuries, the most important being the first—the
Legend of Deer—extending to nineteen lines of continuous
prose. These entries form what we call OLD GAELIC, but the
language is Early Irish of an advanced or phonetically decayed
kind."

The next document is *The Book of the Dean of Lismore*, an
island in Argyllshire, written about 1512 in phonetic Gaelic. We
call it MIDDLE GAELIC (M.G.), a term which also includes the
MSS. of the MacVurich *seanachies*. " The Fearnaig MSS.,
written about 1688, is also phonetic in its spelling, and forms,"
says Dr. MacBain, " a valuable link in the chain of Scottish
Gaelic phonetics from *The Book of Deer* till now." It is simpler
and more characteristic of Celtic Scotland than the eighteenth
century form. The term GAELIC (G.) means modern Gaelic.

The Gaelic alphabet consists of eighteen letters, viz. *a, b, c, d,
e, f, g, h, i, l, m, n, o, p, r, s, t*, and *u*.

Scottish Gaelic printed literature dates from 1567, when John
Carswell issued a translation of Knox's *Liturgy*.

There is a Chair of Celtic Languages and Literature at
Edinburgh University, and a Lectureship of Celtic Languages
and Literature at Glasgow University.

THE HIGHLAND DRESS

AND HOW TO WEAR IT

THE Highland dress as presently worn is the result of a process of evolution. Prior to 1600 the dress of the Gaels of Ireland and Scotland was the *léine-chroich* or saffron shirt. M. Nicolay d'Arfeville, Cosmographer to the King of France, and who visited Scotland in the sixteenth century, writes : " They wear, like the Irish, a large and full shirt, coloured with saffron, and over this a garment hanging to the knee, of thick wool, after the manner of a cassock." About the beginning of the seventeenth century this saffron shirt ceased to be regarded as part of the Highland dress, and the *breacan-féile* or belted plaid and the *féile-beag* or little kilt took its place. The former was a combination of kilt and plaid, and consisted of twelve ells of tartan (six ells of double tartan) neatly plaited and fastened round the body with a belt, the lower part forming the kilt, and the other half being fixed to the shoulder with a brooch, hung down behind and thus formed the plaid. It was possible to display considerable skill and neatness in arranging the plaits, so as to show the sett of the pattern. The *féile-beag* was made of six ells of single tartan, which, being plaited and sewn, was fixed round the waist with a strap, half a yard being left plain at each end, which crossed each other in front. This is really the modern form of that part of the Highland dress.

For everyday wear the Highland dress should consist of a kilt, jacket, and vest of tweed, or what is known as " hill checks," with horn buttons, strong *brogs* or shoes, plain knitted hose, garters, and a bonnet somewhat after the style of the " Balmoral." The sporran should be of leather, or the head of a fox, badger, or other such animal. A plaid about 4 yards long by 1½ wide, and fringed at the ends, is often worn, though of late a Highland cloak or " Inverness cape " has largely superseded the plaid. For day wear the tartan kilt is worn with a tweed jacket and vest. The kilt should be belted round the waist, and should never be worn with braces or straps. The kilt should reach the centre of the knee cap. The best manner of testing this is for the wearer to kneel on the ground. In this position the bottom of the kilt would just touch the ground and no more. The *sgian-dubh* is worn in the stocking, on the outer part of the right leg. The bonnet may contain a brooch showing the crest of the wearer, or a badge consisting of that of his chief within a " belt and buckle " bearing the motto.

9

The *full dress* Highland costume consists of a kilt or *féile-beag* and plaid of some regular tartan, with hose either made from the web of tartan or knitted in check of its prominent colours in the proper propo^tions, a doublet of cloth, velvet, or tartan with lozenge or diamond-shaped silver buttons (if an open doublet is worn, which is that usually affected by civilians, the waistcoat may be of scarlet or white or tartan), low-cut shoes, silver-mounted sporran, and broad bonnet with badge or crest, a brooch to fasten the plaid, a waist-belt, and a baldric or sword-belt ; the arms—a claymore or broadsword, dirk, *sgian-dubh*, a pair of pistols, and a powder-horn.

KILT.—If a member of a clan possessing one or more tartans, such as " clan," " hunting," or " dress," the person should wear his own tartan, either " clan," " hunting," or " dress," or a combination of the first two. Of course on " dress occasions " the " dress " tartan is generally worn. If belonging to a sept of any clan, he should wear the tartan of the clan of which he is a sept, if the sept has no special tartan of its own. If the sept has a special tartan, he should wear it. When the wearer is entitled to both a " clan " and a " district " tartan it is admissible to wear kilt and hose of the latter and doublet or plaid of the former. It is not considered proper to combine either " clan " or " hunting " tartan with " dress " tartan. If one is to wear " dress " tartan, the kilt, plaid, and hose must be uniform.

PLAID.—The long shoulder plaid should be worn. The square shawl plaid, which is more suitable in the ballroom in olden days was sometimes of silk. The hose must correspond with either the kilt or plaid. The long plaid is usually worn over the sword-belt, and removed entirely in the ballroom.

BONNET.—The bonnet should be broad and blue, somewhat akin to what is called the " Balmoral." The " Glengarry " is preferred by the Gordons and some branches of the MacDonald clan. The bonnet should bear the crest and motto of the wearer if he has one, or the chief's crest within a " belt and buckle " surround, without which even a Duke's younger son must not wear his chief's crest, also the evergreen badge of his clan or sept. (*See* illustration following " Urquhart.")

GARTERS.—The garters may be of scarlet, 1–1½ inch in width. There is a special knot, called in Gaelic *snaoim gartain.* Garters with rosettes date from seventeenth–eighteenth century.

DOUBLET.—The jacket or doublet may be of velvet or cloth,

or tartan cut on the bias. The jacket must be of proper Highland pattern. The oldest form is the *côla-geàrr*, something like what is commonly called a " swallow-tail," but cut short in the tails, or even like an ordinary shooting coat, but short, and with Highland pocket flaps and cuffs. The buttons may be round or diamond-shaped, bearing the wearers crest if he has one, or may show cairngorm. The buttoned-up doublet is allied to the military, while the open doublet is favoured by civilians.

SPORRAN.—Goat skin—black, grey, or white—with or without tassels, otter or badger is now more usual. The mounting of the sporran should show the wearer's crest or shield, if armigerous, and the ornamentations thereon should be Celtic in design, corresponding with those on brooch, belt, and buckles.

SHOES.—The shoes must be low cut. Buckles or laces are optional; when such are worn, they must be uniform in ornament with the belts, buckles, etc. For day wear, brown brogues are correct with red-based tartan.

CLAYMORE, SWORD-BELT, AND PISTOLS.—Still worn with court dress and on special occasions of clan ceremonial. Sword-belt, etc., of black or other leather, bearing crested buckles and ornamented with stitching, etc., if desired. Patent leather is modern and objectionable. A double-channelled sword blade with basket hilt, lined with scarlet cloth or tartan to correspond with the dress. Dirk of proper pattern, and bearing Celtic ornamentations. *Sgian-dubh* uniform with dirk in design. Single-barrelled muzzle loading belt pistol of antique pattern, ramrod attached to the barrel. Powder-horn worn on the right side, with the mouth-piece to the front.

ORNAMENTS.—Should be embossed, etched or engraved. They consist of buckles for shoes and belts ; mounting for the sporran, on which is displayed the armorial shield—if wearer is entitled to one—and for a chief " supporters " ; which should also appear on the waist- and sword-belts ; an ornament for the bonnet, on which is shown the proper crest and motto, or clansmen " badge " with the " belt and buckle " ; and a brooch to fasten the plaid, with or without a cairngorm or other stone, and ornamented like the buckles, etc.

LADIES.—For day wear, a kirtle-skirt, cut differently from a man's kilt, with a blouse, tweed or other jacket ; diced or other long stockings *covering the knees* are worn with brogues. The sporran is not worn by ladies, and the travesties of male attire recently worn by dancers at Highland Gatherings are an affront to the nation. Queens, Peeresses, etc., (" sacred embodiments of their races ") though wearing relative robes, do not masquerade in male *garments* ; nor did Highland women.

Celtic women's full dress, or for evening wear, consists of the seventeenth–eighteenth century adaptation of the *arisaid*, viz., a gathered skirt of 3½ yds. very light weight tartan, which may come either just below the knee for high-step dancing, or 4 inches below for other and ballroom dances. From the waist the " plaid " (formerly upper part of the *arisaid*, 1½ × 2 yds. of the tartan), gathered on a concealed belt, falls backwards pannier-wise *on both sides*, and the right-hand corner (8 ins. inwards) is brooched up to the woman's right shoulder, the other corner and fringed edge swinging loose from the shoulder, leaving the *arisaid* sloping diagonally across the back in romantic manner. The lacing-fronted velvet Celtic corsage with braiding and Celtic buttons is laced through holes below each button and worn over a saffron or white " gown " with wide elbow-length sleeves gathered with tartan ribbons and Celtic buttons. Natural nylon stockings, laced shoes, and a snood of tartan ribbon with smallest size crest-brooch in the hair complete this beautiful dress, the Scots woman's national dress. Highland women play the *clarsach* and violin, but *not* bagpipes, which do not display them to advantage and pertain to men.

SASH.—With Lowland evening dress a sash is worn over and brooched on the right shoulder ; only lady-Chiefs, Chieftainesses and wives of Chiefs and Chieftains wear it over the left shoulder. Women married out of the clan wear it over right shoulder and bow-tied on left hip.

GENERAL.—Those not bearing a clan surname or that of any clan sept, should wear a " District " tartan if any suitable one exists, or else " Jacobite " or " Caledonia " tartan, admissible even when the wearer belongs to no clan.

The day dress of vegetable-hued hard tartan, and tweed jacket, is simple and workmanlike. For formal wear the Highland dress naturally lends itself to the glittering ornaments, cairngorms, braiding, and velvet or tartan doublets, which combine with the tartans to enhance that rich variety of costume which accords with the history and instincts of the Highlander. Attempts by self-conscious Lowlanders to convert the picturesque dress of the Gael into a " quiet style " and to deprive the garb of its ornaments or reduce it to the drab monotony of Anglo-Saxon evening clothes are un-Scottish and contemptible.

CLAN CEREMONIAL

The Clan, or Family, like every other institution, requires symbolism and ceremonial, else its existence, functions and tradition get overlooked. It is a legal and practical community—a biological corporation—under its representative—" whom we call Chief "—distinguished by his shield and banner, which pass as property in the ruling line of succession. It spreads into branches and sub-branch families, each with its *ceantighe*. Each child should be taught to " name your chief," the chief's genealogy, and his own. It is the mother's duty to learn this and teach them, the father's to encourage the child to " decor the house," support the chief, and work for the glory of the clan.

There should be three clan, branch and immediate " family " meetings (or at least one of each) every year, to see what can be done to assist and advance kinsfolk. Keep nine family festivals : (1) Christmas, when sovereigns wore their crowns ; (2) Queen's birthday ; (3) St. Andrews Day ; (4) Chief's birthday ; (5) Clan Saint's Day ; (6) The Clan Day—anniversary of charter or exploit ; (7) Chieftain's birthday ; (8) Branch Day ; (9) Birthday of *Ceantighe* of household—father or mother. At clan branches or dinners, toast of the Chief—by name, no ambiguities!—immediately follows Royal Toast.

Chiefs, Chieftains and *duine-uasail* lairds should be careful to use their correct Scoto-lawful name and/or style and signature, especially in all formal or public documents and registrations. They are the key-pieces of the clan structure. At marriages, baptisms and funerals, recall pedigree and exploits and display portraits. Thus, in houses great or small, is tradition handed on. (For more elaborate ceremonial, see *Clans, Septs and Regiments of the Scottish Highlands*, 1965 edition.)

At clan or branch conventions, if the Chief or Chieftain is not present, he may be represented by (a) a Commissioner fully authorised to " hold his place and display his banner " (issued for each special occasion), or (b) an *Ard-Tosachdeor*—the Chief's High Commissioner in some wide area (analogous to the *Ardrigh's* Sheriff)—given authority to display the chief's pinsel—a lesser flag—if he has registered one.

The proceedings, if outdoors, normally commence with a procession to the gathering ground ; if indoors, with a formal procession of entry. Outdoors, a specially appointed officer or particular cadet sometimes has the leading of an advanced-gaurd. The Chief, Chieftain or Chieftainess enters in formal procession, preceded by (1) pipers, (2) *Gilli-brataich* (bannerman), (3) *Cean-*

13

cath with claymore of state, and *Gillisporain* together immediately before the Chief. The Tanist and other officers of the Chief's household and, if the *Ban-tigherna* be with him, her attendants, follow immediately behind the Chief with the Clan magnates and their wives. When arranged in state, the *Gilli-brataich* with the banner stands behind the Chief or Chieftain, and the *Cean-cath* at the Chief's right hand. The *Ban-tigherna* sits at the Chief's left hand. The *Cean-leuchd-tighe* is usually posted near the doorway, but is not the actual door-ward.

The " eldest cadet " or (where the chiefship has passed to or through a female) the heir-male is normally Leader of the right wing, or *Cean-cath*, and is also, as Steward, entrusted with the modern equivalent of " collecting the calps," viz., formally organising or supervising the collection of expenses of the convention. It is the privilege of the clansfolk to meet the expenses of gatherings, the presentation of great-brooch or other gift, furnishing the Chief or Chieftain with banner and claymore, and rematriculating his arms in Lyon Register, on his succession. In days of high taxation the dignity of a clan cannot otherwise be maintained.

At full clan-conventions, when neither the Chief nor his Commissioner is present, his plaid and crested bonnet are carried in by the *Gille-mor*, the bonnet being placed by the *Toisachdeor* beside the plaid on the chiefly-chair.

The Chief or Chieftain's wedding and funeral invitations should bear his/her arms, correct style and titles, and the banner be borne at the ceremony. At a wedding the bridegroom arrives with his banner, that of the bride's father being carried five paces ahead of them. The bridal wreath of a chief's daughter is properly of their plant badge, sometimes silvered, and wedding favours of her father's heraldic livery colours. At a chief's or chieftain's funeral his great-flag is laid on the coffin along with the chief/chieftain's sword, if any, and tartan plaid. Immediately before the coffin are borne claymore, carrying-banner and/or pinsel.

The chief's armorial bearings perform in the clan the same function that the Royal Arms do in a kingdom.

GAELIC NAMES AND SURNAMES

Abbreviations.—Ag.S., Anglo Saxon ; Eng., English ; G., Gaelic ; M.G., Middle Gaelic ; O.G., Old Gaelic ; Gr., Greek ; Heb., Hebrew ; Ir., Irish ; E.Ir., Early Irish ; M.Ir., Middle Irish ; O.Ir., Old Irish ; Lat., Latin ; Fr., French ; Ger., German ; N., Norse ; Sc., Scots. See Chapter on " The Language of the Gael," page 9.

ADAM, G., **Adhamh,** from Heb. *Adam,* red.
ADAMNAN, G. **Adhmhnan** (pr. *yownan*), " little Adam."
ALEXANDER, G. **Alasdair**; Sc. Sandy, fr. Gr. " helper of men." G. **MacAlasdair,** Mac-andie.
ALLAN, G. **Ailean,** from G. *al,* a rock. Hence MacAllan.
ALPIN, G. **Ailpein,** fr. Pictish or Welsh sources.
ANDREW, G. **Aindrea, Gilleanndrias**; Eng. Gillanders, " St Andrew's *gille.*"
ANGUS, G. **Aonghas,** " unique choice."
ARCHIBALD, G. **Gilleasbuig,** " Bishop's *gille,*" Gillespie.
ARTHUR, G. **Artair,** O.Ir., **Art :** Celtic, " high."

BAIN, from G. *bàn,* white. Hence G. **MacGillebhàin,** " Fair *gille* " ; Eng., Whyte, wh. **MacGilvane.**
BARTHOLOMEW, G. **Parlan :** Ir. *Parthalon,* Son of Furrows.
BROWN, G. **Mac-a'-Bhriuthainn :** Ger. *bruno.,* brown. May be G. *brithcamh,* a judge ; Mac-brayne.

CAMERON, G. **Camshron, Camran,** from *cam,* wry, and *sròn* nose—" wry nose." Cf. *Caimbeul* for Campbell.
CAMPBELL, G. **Caimbeul,** from *cam,* wry and *beul,* mouth— " wry mouth."
CARMICHAEL, G. **MacGillemhicheil,** " Son of the *gille* of St. Michael." Carmichael in Lanark, " Seat of Michael."
CATTANACH, CHATTAN, G. **Catanach,** " belonging to Clan Chattan." *Gille-Catan,* " Servant of St. Catan."
CHARLES, G. **Teàrlach;** in origin same as Sc. *carle,* and meaning " man." Hence *MacKerlie,* Sc. Charlie.
CHISHOLM, G. **Siosal, Siosalach,** from place-name Chisholm, Roxburghshire.
CHRISTOPHER. *See* Gilchrist.
CLARK, G. **Cléireach,** G. *cléireach,* a clerk or cleric.
COLIN, G. **Cailean,** evidently from *cuilean,* whelp.
COLL, G. **Colla,** " high " Hence MacColl.

15

CRERAR, G. **Criathrar**, a Loch Tay name, fr. " riddler "—G. *criathar*, to riddle.

CUMMING, G. **Cuimein, Cuimeanach**;   Norman, Comyn.

DAVID, G. **Daibhidh, Dàidh.   Clann Dàidh**, Davidson.

DERMID, G. **Diarmad**;   Ir. *Dermit, Dermot*, " freeman."

DEWAR, G. **Deòir Deòreach**, a custodian.

DONALD, G. **Dòmhnuil**, " world-ruler."

DUFF, M.Ir. **Dubh** (*Clann Dubh*, Clan Duff).

DUFFY. *See Macphee.*

DUGALD, G. **Dùghall**;   M.Ir. *Dubgall*, " Black Stranger."

DUNCAN, G. **Donnchadh**, *donn*, brown, *cath*, a battle—" Brown Warrior."

EDWARD, G. **Éideard, Imhear, Iomhar**, fr. English Edward, Norse *Ivarr*.

EVANDER. *See* MacIver.

EWEN, G. **Eóghan**, " well born, good."   *See* Hugh.

FARQUHAR, G. **Fearchar**, " super-dear one."

FERGUS, G. **Fearghas**, " super-choice."

FINGAL, G. **Fionn**, Macpherson's **Fionnghal**.   *See Fionnaghal*, the Gaelic form of Flora.

FINLAY, G. **Fionnla, Fionnlagh**, " fair-hero."

FORBES, G. **Foirbeis, Foirbeiseach**, fr. *Forbes*, Aberdeenshire.

FRASER, G. **Friseal, Frisealach**, usually referred to O.Fr. *freze*, a strawberry.   Strawberry leaves form part of the Fraser armorial bearings.

GALBRAITH, G. **Mac-a'-Bhreatnaich**, " Son of the Briton."

GEORGE, G. **Seòras, Seòrsa, Deòrsa**, from Gr. " a farmer " or " worker of the earth."   Hence MacGeorge.

GILBERT, G. **Gilleabart, Gillebride**.   Gilbert fr. Ag.S. *Gislebert*, " bright hostage " ;   **Gillebride**, St. Bridget's *gille*.

GILCHRIST, G. **Gillecriosd**, " Servant of Christ."

GILLESPIE, G. **Gilleasbuig**.   *See* Archibald.

GILLIES, G. **Gilliosa**, " Servant of Jesus."   From **Mac-'ill-Ios'** comes the English form Lees, MacLeish.

GLASS, G. **Glas**, " grey."   Hence Macglashan.

GODFREY, G. **Goraidh**;   Ag.S. *Godefrid*, " God's peace."

GORDON, G. **Gòrdan, Gòrdonach**, fr. parish *Gordon*.

GOW, G. **Gobha**, " a smith."   Hence MacGowan.

GRANT, G. **Grannd**.   Originally Englished from " grand."

GREGOR, G. **Griogair**, Lat. *Gregorius*, " watchman."

GUNN, G. **Guinne, Gunnach**;   N. *gunnr*, war.

HAROLD, G. **Harailt**, from N. *Haraldr*, herald.

HECTOR, G. **Eachunn**, " horse lord or horseman."

HENRY, G. **Eanruig**, from O.Eng. Henrie, " home ruler." Hence MacKendrick, Henderson.

HUGH, G. **Uisdean, Huisdean**, in Argyll *Eóghan*.

JAMES, G. **Seumas**, mod. Heb. *Jacob*, supplanter.

JOHN, G. **Iain**, older **Eòin**, " The Lord's Grace."

KATHEL, G. **Cathal**. Hence MacCathail, MacCall, MacKail.

KENNEDY, G. **Ceannaideach, Ceanadaidh** ; E.Ir. *Cennetich* " ugly head."

KENNETH, G. **Coinneach**, " fire-sprung." Cf. **MacCoinnich**.

LACHLAN, G. **Lachunn, Lachlann**, N. *Lochlann*, " Fjordland."

LAMOND, G. **MacLaomuinn**, fr. N. " lawman " ; MacClymont.

LAURENCE, G. **Labhruinn**, Lat. *Laurentius*, St. Lawrence—Lat. *laurus*, a laurel.

LEWIS, G. **Luthais**, Fr. *Louis*. See Eng. Ludovick.

LIVINGSTONE, G. **Mac-an-leigh**. *See* Macleay.

LUDOVICK, G. **Maoldònuich**, " Shaveling of the Church." Ludovick is from Ludwig, O.Ger. *Chlodwig*.

LUKE, G. **Lùcais**. Hence G. **MacLùcais**, MacLucas.

MACASKILL, G. **MacAsgaill**, fr. N. *Askell* for *As-ketill*, (" vessel of holiness ").

MACAULAY, G. **MacAmhlaidh**, from N. *Oláfr*.

MACBEAN, G. **MacBheathain**, G. *Beathan*, " Life's Son."

MACBETH, G. **Macbheatha, MacBheathaig**, " Son of Life."

MACCAIG, G. **MacCaog**, Ir. *MacTaidhg*, Son of Teague.

MACCALLUM, G. **MacCaluim**. *See* Malcolm.

MACCODRUM, G. **MacCodrum**, N. *Guttormr*; Ag.S. *Guthrum*, " good or god serpent."

MACCOMBIE, G. **Comaidh**, Tommie, Thomas.

MACCONACHIE, G. **MacDhonnchaidh**, " Son of Duncan."

MACCORMIC, G. **Cormaig**, fr. E.Ir. *Cormac* or *Cormag*, charioteer.

MACCORQUODALE, G. **MacCòrcadail**, from N. *Thorketill*, Thor's kettle or holy vessel. *See* MacAskill.

MACCOWAN, G. **MacCòmhghan**, from St. Cowan ; may also be from Sc. *cowan*, a dike-builder.

MACCRIMMON, G. **MacCruimein**, from *Ruman* (on a Manx inscription) ; from N. *Hromundr*, " famed protector."

MACCULLOCH, G. **MacCullach**, " Son of the Boar."

MACECHERN, G. **MacEachairn**, " horse lord," from G. *each* and *tighearna*; also Englished Mackechnie.

MacFADYEN, G. **MacPhàidein**, G. *Pàidean*, Patrick.

MacGILL, G. **MacGille**, son of the servant.

MacGILLIVRAY, G. **MacGillebhrath**, " Son of the Servant of Judgment," from G. *bràth*, judgment.

MacGLASHAN, G. **Glaisein, Gilleghlais**, " The Grey Lad."

MacHARDY, G. **MacCàrdaidh**—a sept of the Farquharsons.

MacINTYRE, G. **Mac-an-t-saoir**, " Son of the Carpenter."

MacISAAC. *See* MacKessack.

MacIVER, G. **MacIamhair**, from N. *Ivarr*. *See* Edward.

MacKAY, G. **MacAoidh**, from *Aoidh*; O.G. *Æd*, firebrand.

MacKELLAR, G. **MacEalair**; Ir. *Elair*, Lat. *Hilarius*.

MacKESSACK, G. **MacCesaig, Mackessoc**, St. Kessog.

MacKILLOP, G. **MacPhilip**, from Gr. " lover of horses."

MacKINLAY, G. **MacFhionnlaigh**; from Finlay.

MacKINNON, G. **MacFhionghuin**, son of Fingon, " fair born " ; also written Mackinven.

MacKINTOSH, G. **Mac-an-tòisich**, " The Son of the Thane," or G. *tòiseach*. Hence Tosh.

MacKIRDY, G. **MacUrardaigh**, " sea-director " ; whence MacMurtrie and MacMutrie.

MacLAGAN, G. **MacLagain** or **MacLathagain**.

MacLAREN, G. **MacLabhruinn**. *See* Laurence.

MacLARTY, G. **MacLabhartaigh**, from G. *Flaithbheartach* Eng. *Flaherty*, " dominion bearing."

MacLAUCHLAN, G. **MacLachainn**. *See* Lachlan.

MacLEAN, G. **MacGilleathain** for Gill'Sheathain, " John or *Seathan's* Servant " ; " Son of the Servant of John."

MacLEARNAN, G. **MacGill'Ernan**, " St. Ernan's *gille*."

MacLEAY, G. **Mac-an-léigh**; Ir. *Donnsléibhe*. The Macleays of Lorn Englished as Livingstone.

MacLELLAN, G. **MacGillhfaolain**, " St. Fillan's Servant."

MacLENNAN, G. **MacGillfhinnein**, " Servant of St. Finnan."

MacLEOD, G. **MacLeòid**; O.G. *Léot* ; Norse Sagas, *Ljótr*.

MacMAHON, G. **MacMhathain**. *See* Matheson.

MacMARTIN, G. **MacMhàirtin**, earlier **Gillemàrtain**.

MacMASTER, G. **Mac-a'-Mhaighster**, " Son of the Master."

MacMICHAEL, G. **MacMhicheil**, doubtless for *Gillemichol*.

MacMILLAN, G. **MacMhaolain**, " Son of the Bald *gille*."

MacNAB, G. **Mac-an-Aba**, " Son of the Abbot."

MacNAIR, G. **Mac-an-Uidhir** for **Mac Iain uidhir**, " Son of the Dun (*odhar*) John." In Perth and Lennox, is from G. *Mac-an-oighre*, " Son of the Heir," and they are regarded as a sept of Clan Farlane.

MacNAUGHTON, G. **MacNeachdain** ; O.G. *Nectan*.

MacNEE, G. **MacRigh**, " Son of a King."

MacNICOL, G. **Neacail**, Lat. *Nicolas*, " conquering people."

MacNish, G. **MacNeis**, G. *MacNaois*, a form of Angus.
MacNiven, G. **MacGille-naoimh**, " The Saintly *gille*."
MacPhail, G. **MacPhàil**, " Son of Paul." *See* Paul.
Macphee, G. **Mac-a-Phi**. MacDuffie for *MacDubh-sìthe*.
Macpherson, G. **Mac-a'-Phearsain**, " Son of the Parson."
Macquarrie, G. **MacGuaire** ; E.Ir. *guaire*, noble.
Macqueen, G. **MacCuine** for **MacShuibhne**, N. *Sweyn*.
Macrae, G. **MacRath**, " Son of Grace or Luck."
Macraild. *See* Harold.
MacTaggart, G. **Mac-an-t-Sagairt**, " Son of the Priest."
MacTavish, G. **MacThàimhs, MacThamhais**, " Son of Thomas."
MacVicar, G. **MacBhiocair**, " Son of the Vicar."
MacVurich, G. **MacMhuirich**. Bardic family claimed descent from *Muireach Albannach*. They now call themselves Macphersons.
Magnus, G. **Manus**; Lat. *magnus*, great.
Malcolm, G. **Calum**, earlier **Gillecalum**; Ir. *Maelcoluim*, fr. *maol*, bald, and *calum*, a dove—St. Columba.
Malise, G. **Maol Iosa**, " Servant of Jesus."
Martin, Eng. Martin, Lat. *Martinus*, martial.
Matheson, G. **MacMhathan, Mathanach**; Ir. *Macmahon*. " Son of the Bear." Mathew-son, G. **MacMhatha**.
Menzies, G. **Mèinn, Mèinnear, Mèinnearach**, from Fr. " of the household "—*De Meyners*.
Morgan, G. **Morgunn**, *Clann Mhic Mhorguinn*, Pictish, *Morgund*.
Morrison, G. **Moireasdan, MacGille-Mhoire**, " Mary's Servant " ; M.G. *Gillamure*, whence Gilmour.
Munro, G. **Rothach, Mac-an-Rothaich**.
Murdoch, G. **Muireach, Murchadh**, two names from different roots. **Muireach**, " lord, king," **Murchadh**, " sea king." From the first, **MacMhuirich**; from second Murchison, Murchie, and Ir. Murphy.
Murray, G. **Moirreach**, from the county name Moray.
Myles, G. **Maol-Moire**, " Servant of Mary."

Neil, G. **Niall**, " champion." Hence MacNeill, Nelson.
Nicolson, G. **MacNeacail**. *See* MacNicol.
Norman, G. **Tormoid, Tormod**, N. " Thor protection."

Patrick, G. **Pàdruig, Pàruig**; pet form, **Para**.
Paul, G. **Pòl** : classic form **Pàl** from Lat. *paulus*, small.
Peter, G. **Peadair**, from Lat. *petrus*, rock.
Philip, *See* MacKillop.

RANALD, G. **Raonull**, N. *Rögnvaldr*, ruler of the gods.
ROBERT, G. **Raibeart**, Ag.S. *Robert*, " bright fame."
RODERICK, RORY, G. **Ruairidh**, " famed ruler."
ROSS, G. **Rosach**, from G. *ros*, a promontory.
ROY, G. **Ruadh**, red. Hence Macinroy.

SAMUEL, G. **Somhairle**, from Somerled, " summer sailor."
SHAW, G. **Seadhgh**, " strong one." In Argyll the Shaws are
    called *Clann Mhic-gille-Sheathanaich*.
SIMON, G. **Sim**. Hence **MacShimidh**, Lord Lovat.
SOMERLED. *See* Samuel.
SUTHERLAND, G. **Sutherlanach**, from the county name.

TAGGART, *See* MacTaggart.
THOMAS, G. **Tómas, Tàmhas**. Also MacTavish, MacCombie.
TORQUIL, G. **Torcull** or **Torcall**, N. *Thorkell, Thor ketill*.

WHYTE, G. **MacGillebhàin**, " Son of the fair *gille*."
WILLIAM, G. **Uilleam**. Hence MacWilliam.

Until the mid-nineteenth century names were spelt hap-
hazardly and this resulted in many variations. Clansfolk should
keep this in mind and not expect to find uniformity.

FEMALE PERSONAL NAMES

ANN, G. **Anna**, from Heb. " grace."
ANNABELLA, G. **Anabladh**, from Heb. " eagle heroine."
BARBARA, G. **Barbara**; Gr. " stranger."
BESSIE, BETTY. *See* Elizabeth.
BETHIA, G. **Beathag**, " life," from Gr. *beatha*.
BRIDGET, G. **Bride**, " strength."
CATHERINE, G. **Catriona** ; Gr. " pure."
CECILIA, G. **Sileas** : Lat. " blind." Englished as *Shiela*.
CHRISTINA, G. **Cairistiona** ; Gr. " Christian."
CLARA, G. **Sorcha**, " bright."
DOROTHY, G. **Diorbhàil, Diorbhoguil**, " Gift of God."
ELIZABETH, G. **Ealasaid**; Heb. " Oath of God."
ELLEN or HELEN, G. **Eilidh**; Gr. " light."
EUPHEMIA (EFFIE), G. **Aoirig, Eighrig** ; M.G. *Effric*.
FLORA, G. **Fionnaghal, Flòraidh**, " flowers " ; Sc. Flory.
    Also G. *Finvola*, fair shouldered, G. *Fionn-ghuala*.
FRANCES, G. **Frangag**, " free."
GRACE, G. **Giorsal** ; Lat. " grace."
ISABELLA, G. **Iseabel**, from Heb. " Oath of God."
JANE, JEAN, G. **Sine**, from Heb. " Grace of the Lord."
JANET, G. **Seònaid**, Perths. **Deònaid** ; " Grace of the Lord."
JULIA, G. **Sileas**. *See* Cecilia.
KATE, G. **Ceit**; Gr. " pure."
LILIAS, G. **Lileas**.
LUCY, G. **Liusaidh** ; Lat. " light."
MARGARET (MAGGIE), G. **Mairghread, Peigi** ; Gr. " pearl."
MARION. *See* Muriel. Heb. " bitter."
MARJORY, G. **Marsali** ; Gr. " pearl." Pet form May.
MARY, G. **Màiri, Moire**, or **Muire** ; Heb. " bitter."
MOLLY, G. **Malai** ; Heb. " bitter." Pet form of Mary.
MURIEL, G. **Muireall**, Gr. " myrrh."
RACHAEL, G. **Raoghnailt, Raonaild, Raonaid** ; from N.
    Raghildr, " God's fight."
SARAH (SALLY), G. **Mór, Mórag**, from G. *mór*, great. Sarah is
    from Heb., and means " queen."
SOPHIA, G. **Beathag** ; Gr. " wisdom."
SUSAN, G. **Siùsaidh** ; Heb. " lily."
WINIFRED, G. **Una**, " white stream."

In Gaelic surnames the feminine equivalent of the masculine
mac, son of, is *nic*, daughter of, and so in description (as distinct
from a *name*) *mac* surnames take *nic* when prefixed by a female
personal name. " Mairi-*nic*-Dhòmhnuill " is Mary the daughter
of Donald.

CHIEFSHIP AND CHIEFTAINCY

The chief is the " Representer " of the ancestor who founded the clan or family and has been defined as " the Sacred Embodiment of the Race." The Ard-Righ, as a tribal sovereignty, is the supreme chiefship differing from others only in degree. The early inauguration ceremonies were analogous (*Scottish Coronations*, 16) and the King of Scots hailed Chief in his coronation. W. F. Skene, Historiographer-Royal, says chiefship is by nature hereditary, and not always synonymous with war-leader. Before lineal succession was evolved, the King or Chief nominated or selected his successor from a *derbhfine* group of nine next of kin—which in Scotland could include descendants through females. To prevent interregnum and bloody disputes when the King or Chief died without having nominated a Tanist, a law attributed to King Malcolm MacKenneth fixed as the line of succession : " son or daughter, grandson or granddaughter, whom failing the nearest of the Royal or collateral stock." In 1292 the eighty Scots " tryours " of the Centumviral Court-*tribal* (*S.H.R.*, xvi. 7) reported the same order of succession applied to Crown, Earldoms, baronies and impartible tenures (*i.e.* heritable offices). Chiefship descended with the *duthus*—principal estate—and the earliest *barones Scotiæ* were just *Capitani tribuum* (*i.e.* chiefs). " By the law of Scotland heritages of all kinds, including alike lands and honours, descend at common law to heirs-of-line, not heirs male " (Lord Lyon Burnett, *Red Book of Menteith Reviewed*, 49).

The succession is accordingly (as old rulings of the Scots Privy Council and Lyons indicate) analogous to our ancient Scots Law of Heritage, but where Chiefship passes to or through a female, her husband (Chief " by the courtesy of Scotland ") and children *must* take *her* clan-name, failing which it passes to the heir-male. This rule is stated by seventeenth-century lawyers, as the law and custom of Scotland. Each chief has, however, power to nominate, by *Tanistry*, amongst his heirs, a chief, who then succeeds instead of the heirs-at-law. The *Tanist* (nominee) has to petition the Lord Lyon (High Sennachie) for rematriculation of the Chief's Ensign Armorial.

Chieftain is a strictly territorial title, always related to a *place*, and defined (Statute, 1587) as " chiftane of the cuntrie." It is often applied to branch-chiefs since a branch was usually founded by securing a feu-holding. The feminine is " Chieftainess." This and the territorial connection is shown from ancient records.

22

ARMORIAL BEARINGS

Armorial shields and banners are the insignia of chiefs, chieftains and *duine-uasal*. The control of coats of arms and genealogies in Scotland, also official recognition of change of names and designations, lies with the *Court of the Lord Lyon King of Arms, H.M. Register House, Edinburgh*. This represents the Court of the High Sennachie of the Royal House of Scotland. By Acts of the Scots Parliament, 1592 and 1672, arms and crests may only be used by those for whom such have been recorded in the *Public Register of All Arms and Bearings in Scotland*, the registration fees, payable to H.M. Exchequer, being about £60 for a new grant of arms, and £19 for a "matriculation" of the same arms with a "bordure" or other difference showing applicant's relationship to the holder of the principal arms. Arms descend indivisibly and like a peerage—or the Crown, as Sir G. Mackenzie says. Overseas readers please note : No Mr. McSnooks can bear arms of a relative named McBuggins. *Name and Arms* are inseparable and the *undifferenced arms* indicate the chief or chieftain as an officially recognised " public person " in the Scottish realm. If there is no tailzie or destination, arms pass to the heir-of-line, *not* the heir-male, who, as " Representer " (*i.e.* Chief, per Sir G. Mackenzie) confers the " courtesy " of the arms on her husband and transmits the arms undifferenced and unquartered. Keeping the *Name* inherited with the arms is regarded an indispensable condition. The heiress-of-line gets *the crest and supporters*. Rematriculation on succession to " make up title " is a statutory requisite. No one can possess a " crest " without also being in right of a *scutcheon*. A clansman may wear *his chief's* crest within a coiled " belt and buckle " with motto. This shows the use is as clansman, not as owner of the crest. Only the chief, his wife and heir wear the brooch of the complete arms. Clansfolk do *not* put the chief's arms on their stationery. If his crest is used on clan-stationery it must be within the " belt and buckle " *and* accompanied by the words *Girean Ceanncinnidh*. Arms denote the chief, chieftain or *duine uasal* who registered them. It is illegal and " bad taste " for others to use them except in wearing the " belt and buckle " badge. Heraldry has always been closely connected with clanship and Highland dress, ornaments, embroidery banners of chiefs and chieftains, pipe banners, as well as plate, houses, and monuments. Full details of law and practice will be found in *Scots Heraldry* (Oliver & Boyd, 1955). Such works should be consulted or inquiry addressed to the Lyon Court, H.M. Register House (Edinburgh) before money is spent on heraldic decoration.

DESIGNATIONS OF CHIEFS

A number of the following list are Gaelic patronymics, others are territorial, for by Scots law each proprietor of an estate is entitled to add the name of his property to his surname, and if he does this consistently, to treat the whole as a " title " and under Statute (1672, cap. 47) to subscribe himself so. The Lord Advocate obtained a judgment of the Court of Session in 1749, that such titles are " ordinary names." not descriptions of ownership. The Chief of a landed family, whose surname and title both came from his land, was known as, *e.g. Udny of that ilk*, which thus came to imply chiefship. Chiefs of clans, in order to emphasise their chiefship, adopted the same style, but (though " of that ilk " is the older and strictly Scottish style) nowadays often reduplicate the patronymic, *e.g. Macleod of Macleod*. Chiefs were normally styled, *e.g.* " The Laird of Macleod." The prefix, " The Much Honoured," briefly " The," is in Scots, applied to chiefs (a translation of mediaeval " Le," *e.g.* " Le Graham "). But at home, in the *duthus*, " The MacSporran " is referred to as " MacSporran."

The wives and unmarried daughters of chiefs, chieftains, and lairds are entitled to use these " titles," and the heir prefixes the word " younger," but only the head of the house, his wife and heir use the style " of that ilk." *e.g.* " MacTavish of that Ilk," " Mrs. MacTavish of that Ilk," " Ian MacTavish younger of that Ilk," "Miss Jean MacTavish of MacTavish." But a chief or laird's wife is still properly styled, *e.g.* " Lady MacTavish " and addressed as " *Mo Ban-tigherna*." In personal address the title alone is used, *e.g.* " MacKinnon " or " Locheil " (no " Mr."), and, in both speech and writing, a laird or chieftain should be addressed by the name of his estate, *not* as " Mr. X—." In writing, " Esq," if added, follows after the designation (see T. Innes of Learney, *Tartans of the Clans and Families of Scotland*, p. 61 ; *Clans, Septs and Regiments of Scottish Highlands*, p. 396.)

Celtic Designation.			Scottish Equivalent.
Am Mèinnearach*	.	.	Menzies of that Ilk.
Am Moirreach Mór	.	.	Murray Duke of Atholl.
An Drumanach Mór	.	.	The Earl of Perth (Drummond).
An Gòrdanach*	.	.	Chief of the Gordons (Marquis of Huntly).
An Granntach*	.	.	Grant of Grant (Lord Strathspey).
An Greumach Mór	.	.	The Duke of Montrose (The Graham).
An Siosalach*	.	.	The Chisholm.
An t-Ailpeanach	.	.	MacGregor of MacGregor.
Clan Theàrlaich Buidhe	.	.	Macleans of Dochgarroch.
Clannfhearghuis Srath-churra			Ferguson of Strachur.
Donnachadh Reamhar Mac-Aonghuis	.	.	Robertsons of Struan (Struan-Robertson).
Gillichattan Mór	.	.	Mackintosh of Clan Chattan.
MacPharthaloin	.	.	MacFarlane of that Ilk.
Mac-a'-PhiCholosaidh	.	.	Macphee of Colonsay.
Mac-an-Aba	.	.	Macnab of Macnab.
Mac'ic-Adam	.	.	Ferguson of Balmacruchie.
Mac-an-Lamhaich	.	.	Lennie of that Ilk.
Mac-an-Leistear	.	.	Fletcher of Achallader.
Mac-Iain-Riabhaich	.	.	Campbell of Ardkinglass.
Mac-an-Tòisich	.	.	The Mackintosh.
Mac-Aoidh (*Moirear Maghrath*)			Lord Reay (The Mackay).
Mac-Aoidh na Ranna	.	.	Mackay of Rhinns (Islay).
MacAonghuis an Dùin	.	.	Campbell of Dunstaffnage.
MacCailein-Mór	.	.	Campbell, Duke of Argyll.
Mac-Chailein-'ic Dhonnachaidh			Campbell of Glenorchy (Earl of Breadalbane).
MacAomalan	.	.	Bannatyne of that Ilk.
Mac-Coinnich*	.	.	MacKenzie of Seaforth.

* Normal use ; technically Mór should be added.

Celtic Designation.	Scottish Equivalent.
MacDhonnachaidh . .	Campbell of Inverawe.
Mac-Cuaire (or Mac-Ghuaire)	Macquarrie of Ulva.
Mac-Dhòmnuill Duibh .	Cameron of Locheil
Mac-Dhòmnuill . .	Macdonald of Macdonald.
Mac-Dhòmnuill-nan-Eilean .	MacDonald of the Isles.
Mac-Dhùgaill Lathurna .	MacDougall of Lorn.
Mac-Dhùgaill Chraignis .	Campbell of Craignish.
MacFhearghuis Dunfalandaidh	Ferguson of Dunfallandy.
Mac-Fhionghuin . . .	Mackinnon of Mackinnon.
Mac Fhionnlaigh . .	Farquharson of Inver cauld.
MacGaradh Mór . . .	Chief of the Hays.
Mac-Gill-onaidh . .	Cameron of Strone.
Mac-Iain	MacDonald of Glencoe.
Mac-Iain-Abrach . .	Maclean of Coll.
Mac-Iain Aird-nam-Murchan .	MacDonald of Ardna-murchan.
Mac-Iain-Duibh . . .	MacAlister of Loup.
Mac-Iain-Oig . . .	MacDonald of Glenalladale.
Mac-Iain Stiubhairt na h-Apunn	Stewart of Appin.
Mac-'ic-Ailein[1] . . .	MacDonald of Clanranald.
Mac-'ic-Alasdair . .	MacDonell of Glengarry.
Mac-'ic-Artair . . .	Campbell of Strachur (MacArthur).
Mac-'ic-Dhùgaill (Mhorair) .	MacDonald of Morar.
Mac-'ic Eachuinn-Chinnghearr-loch	Maclean of Kingerloch.
Mac-Eoghainn-'ic-Eoghainn .	Cameron of Erracht.
Mac-'ic-Eóghain . .	Maclean of Lazonby.
Mac-'ic-Iain . . .	MacKenzie of Gairloch.
Mac-'ic-Mhurchaidh . .	MacKenzie of Achilty.

[1] The style *Mac-'ic* used by certain persons in these families is *not* a " chiefly " title, but actually denotes a *cadet* of the line of the affixed name (*Loyall Dissuasive*, 102), usually applied when the person was *not* actual chief or chieftain.

Celtic Designation.	Scottish Equivalent.
Mac-'ic-Raonuill	MacDonell of Keppoch.
Mac-'ic-Bhaltair	Stewart of Ardvorlich.
Mac-ill-Eathain Dhubhart	Maclean of that Ilk.
Mac-ill-Eathain Lochabuidhe (Sliochd Mhurchaidh Ruaidh)	Maclaine of Lochbuie (race of Murdoch Roy).
Mac-'ille-Chaluim	MacLeod of Raasay.
Mac-'ille-Mhoire	Morrison of Lewis.
Mac-Iomhair	Campbell of Asknish.
Mac-Laomuinn*	Lamont of Lamont.
MacLeòid	MacLeod of Harris.
Mac-mhaoilein-mór-a'-Chnaip	Macmillan of Knap.
Mac-'ic Mhàrtainn	Cameron of Letterfinlay (MacMartin).
MacMhuirich (Cluanaigh)	Macpherson of Cluny.
MacNèill	MacNeil of Barra.
Mac-Phàdruig	Grant of Glenmoriston.
Mac-Sheumais-Chataich	Gunn of Kilearnan.
MacShimidh	Lord Fraser of Lovat.
MacUisdein	Fraser of Culbekie.
Morair Chat	Chief of Clan Sutherland.
Morair Ghallaobh	Earl of Caithness (Sinclair).
Sliochd a' Chlaidheimh Iaruinn	Macleans of Ross of Mull.
Sliochd Phàra Bhig	Campbells of Barcaldine and Baileveolan.
Tighearna Folais	Munro of Foulis.

CLAN SEPTS AND DEPENDENTS

(Name spelling was haphazard until mid-nineteenth century.)

Sept.				Clan.
Abbot	.	.	.	Macnab.
Abbotson	.	.	.	Do.
Abernethy	.	.	.	Leslie.
Adam	.	.	.	Gordon.
Adamson	.	.	.	Mackintosh.
Adie	.	.	.	Gordon.
Airlie	.	.	.	Ogilvie.
Alexander	.	.	.	MacAlister, MacDonald Mac-Donell of Glengarry.
Allan	.	.	.	MacDonald of Clanranald, Mac-Farlane.
Allanson	.	.	.	Do. do.
Allardice	.	.	.	Graham of Menteith.
Alpin	.	.	.	MacAlpine.
Anderson	.	.	.	Anderson.
Andrew	.	.	.	Do.
Angus	.	.	.	Macinnes.
Armstrong	.	.	.	Armstrong.
Arthur	.	.	.	MacArthur or Campbell of Strachur.
Ayson	.	.	.	Mackintosh (Shaw).
Bain	.	.	.	Mackay.
Baird	.	.	.	Baird.
Bannatyne	.	.	.	Campbell of Argyll Stuart of Bute.
Bannerman	.	.	.	Forbes.
Barclay	.	.	.	Barclay.
Bard	.	.	.	Baird.
Bartholomew	.	.	.	MacFarlane.
Baxter	.	.	.	Macmillan.
Bayne	.	.	.	Mackay.
Bean	.	.	.	MacBean.
Beaht	.	.	.	MacDonald, Maclean of Duart.
Beaton	.	.	.	MacDonald, Maclean of Duart, MacLeod of Harris.

28

Sept.	Clan.
Bell	Macmillan.
Berkeley	Barclay.
Bethune	MacDonald, MacLeod of Harris.
Beton	Do. do.
Black	Lamont, MacGregor, Maclean of Duart.
Bontein, Bontine, Buntain, Bunten, Buntine	Graham of Menteith.
Bouchannane	Buchanan.
Boyd	Stewart (Royal).
Brebner, Bremner	Farquharson.
Brieve	Morrison.
Brodie	Brodie.
Brown	Lamont, Macmillan.
Bruce, Brus	Bruce.
Buchan	Cumin.
Buchanan	Buchanan.
Burdon, Bourdon	Lamont.
Burness	Campbell.
Burnett	Do.
Burns	Do.
Caddell	Campbell of Cawdor.
Caird	Sinclair.
Calder	Campbell of Cawdor.
Callum	MacLeod of Raasay.
Cambell	Campbell of Argyll.
Cameron	Cameron.
Campbell	Campbell of Argyll.
Cariston	Skene.
Carmichael	Stewart (Appin, Galloway).
Carnegie	Carnegie.
Carnie	Leslie, Skene.
Cattanach	Clan Chattan.
Caw	MacFarlane.
Chalmers	Cameron.
Cheseholme	Chisholm.
Cheyne	Sutherland.
Chisholm	Chisholm.
Chisholme	Chisholm.
Clark or Clarke	Cameron, Mackintosh, Macpherson.
Clarkson	Do. do.
Clergy	Clergy.

Sept.			Clan.
Clerk	.	.	Cameron, Mackintosh, Macpherson.
Clyne	.	.	Sinclair.
Cockburn	.	.	Cockburn.
Collier	.	.	Robertson.
Colman	.	.	Buchanan.
Colquhoun	.	.	Colquhoun.
Colson	.	.	MacDonald.
Colyear	.	.	Robertson.
Combich	.	.	Stewart of Appin.
Combie	.	.	Mackintosh.
Comrie	.	.	MacGregor or MacGrigor.
Comyn	.	.	Cumin.
Conacher	.	.	MacDougall.
Connall	.	.	MacDonald.
Connell	.	.	Do.
Conochie	.	.	Campbell of Inverawe.
Coulson	.	.	MacDonald.
Coutts	.	.	Farquharson.
Cowan	.	.	Colquhoun, MacDougall.
Cranston	.	.	Cranston.
Crauford	.	.	Crawford.
Craufurd	.	.	Do.
Crawford	.	.	Do.
Crerar	.	.	Mackintosh.
Crookshank	.	:	Stewart of Garth.
Culchone	.	.	Colquhoun.
Cumin or Cummin	.	Cumin.
Cumming	.	.	Do.
Cumyn	.	.	Do.
Cunningham	.	.	Cunningham.
Currie	.	.	MacDonald of Clanranald, Macpherson.
Dallas	.	.	Mackintosh.
Dalyell	.	.	Dalzell.
Dalziel	.	.	Do.
Darroch	.	.	MacDonald.
Davidson	.	.	Davidson.
Davie	.	.	Davidson.
Davis, Davison	.	.	Do.
Dawson	.	.	Do.
Denoon	.	.	Ross.
Denune	.	.	Do.
Deuchar	.	.	Lindsay.

Sept.				Clan.
Dewar	.	.	.	Menzies, Macnab.
Dingwall	.	.	.	Munro, Ross.
Dinnes	.	.	.	Innes.
Dis or Dise	.	.	.	Skene.
Doles	.	.	.	Mackintosh.
Donachie	.	.	.	Robertson.
Donald	.	.	.	MacDonald.
Donaldson	.	.	.	Do.
Donillson	.	.	.	MacDonald (of Antrim).
Donleavy	.	.	.	Buchanan.
Donlevy	.	.	.	Do.
Donnellson	.	.	.	MacDonald (of Antrim).
Dougall	.	.	.	MacDougall.
Douglas	.	.	.	Douglas.
Dove	.	.	.	Buchanan.
Dow	.	.	.	Buchanan, Davidson.
Dowall	.	.	.	MacDougall.
Dowe	.	.	.	Buchanan.
Dowell	.	.	.	MacDougall.
Drummond	.	.	.	Drummond.
Duff	.	.	.	Duff.
Duffie or Duffy	.	.	.	Macfie.
Duilach	.	.	.	Stewart of Garth.
Dunbar	.	.	.	Dunbar.
Duncan	.	.	.	Robertson.
Duncanson	.	.	.	Do.
Dundas	.	.	.	Dundas.
Dunnachie	.	.	.	Robertson.
Dyce or Dys	.	.	.	Skene.
Edie	.	.	.	Gordon.
Elder	.	.	.	Mackintosh.
Elliot	.	.	.	Elliot.
Erskine	.	.	.	Erskine.
Esson	.	.	.	Mackintosh (Shaw).
Ewan	.	.	.	MacLachan.
Ewen	.	.	.	Do.
Ewing	.	.	.	Do.
Farquhar	.	.	.	Farquharson.
Farquharson	.	.	.	Farquharson.
Federith	.	.	.	Sutherland.
Fergus	.	.	.	Ferguson.
Ferguson	.	.	.	Do.
Fergusson	.	.	.	Do.

Sept.			Clan.
Ferries	.	.	Ferguson.
Fersen .	.	.	Macpherson.
Fife .	.	.	MacDuff or Duff.
Findlay	.	.	Farquharson.
Findlayson	.	.	Do.
Finlay	.	.	Do.
Finlayson	.	.	Do.
Fleming	.	.	Murray.
Fletcher	.	.	MacGregor.
Forbes .	.	.	Forbes.
Fordyce	.	.	Do.
Foulis .	.	.	Munro.
France .	.	.	Stewart.
Fraser	.	.	Fraser.
Frazer	.	.	Do.
Fresell .	.	.	Fraser.
Freser	.	.	Do.
Frezel or Frizel	.	.	Do.
Friseal .	.	.	Do.
Frissell or Frizell	.	.	Do.
Fuilarton	.	.	Stuart of Bute.
Fullerton	.	.	Do.
Fyfe .	.	.	MacDuff or Duff.
Galbraith	.	.	MacDonald, MacFarlane.
Gallie .	.	.	Gunn.
Garrow	.	.	Stewart.
Gaunson	.	.	Gunn.
George, Georgeson	.	Do.
Gibb .	.	.	Buchanan.
Gibson .	.	.	Do.
Gilbert .	.	.	Do.
Gilbertson	.	.	Do.
Gilbride	.	.	MacDonald.
Gilchrist	.	.	MacLachlan, Ogilvie.
Gilfillan	.	.	Macnab.
Gillanders	.	.	Ross.
Gillespie	.	.	Macpherson.
Gillies .	.	.	Do.
Gilmore	.	.	Morrison.
Gilroy .	.	.	Grant of Glenmoriston, Mac-Gillivray.
Glen .	.	.	Mackintosh.
Glennie .	.	.	Do.
Gordon	.	.	Gordon.

Sept.	Clan.
Gorrie	MacDonald.
Gow	Macpherson.
Gowan	MacDonald.
Gowrie	Do.
Graeme of Menteith	Graham of Menteith.
Graham	Graham of Montrose.
Grant	Grant.
Grassich	Farquharson.
Gray	Stewart of Athole, Sutherland.
Gregor, Gregorson	MacGregor.
Gregory	Do.
Greig	Do.
Grevsach	Farquharson.
Grier	MacGregor.
Grierson	Do.
Griesck	MacFarlane.
Grigor	MacGregor.
Gruamach	MacFarlane.
Gunn	Gunn.
Hallyard	Skene.
Hamilton	Hamilton.
Hanna, Hannah, Hannay	Hannay.
Hardie	Farquharson, Mackintosh.
Hardy	Do. do.
Harper, Harperson	Buchanan.
Hawes	Campbell.
Haws	Do.
Hawson	Do.
Hawthorn	MacDonald.
Hay	Hay.
Henderson	Gunn, MacDonald of Glencoe (MacIan).
Hendrie	MacNaughton.
Hendry	Do.
Hewison	MacDonald.
Home, Hume	Home.
Houston	MacDonald.
Howison	Do.
Hughson	Do.
Huntly	Gordon.
Hutcheonson	MacDonald.
Hutcheson	Do.
Hutchinson	Do.
Hutchison	Do.

	Sept.			Clan.
Inches	.	.	.	Robertson.
Innes	.	.	.	Innes.
Innie	.	.	.	Do.
Isles	.	.	.	MacDonald.
Jameson	.	.	.	Gunn, Stuart of Bute.
Jamieson	.	.	.	Do. do.
Johnson	.	.	.	Gunn, MacDonald (MacIan), of Ardnamurchan, and of Glencoe.
Johnston	.	.	.	Johnstone.
Johnstone	.	.	.	Do.
Johnstoun	.	.	.	Do.
Kay	.	.	.	Davidson.
Kean	.	.	.	Gunn, MacDonald (MacIan), of Ardnamurchan, and of Glencoe.
Keene	.	.	.	Do. do.
Keith	.	.	.	Keith.
Kellie	.	.	.	MacDonald.
Kelly	.	.	.	Do.
Kendrick	.	.	.	MacNaughton.
Kennedy	.	.	.	Kennedy.
Kenneth	.	.	.	MacKenzie.
Kennethson	.	.	.	Do.
Kerr	.	.	.	Kerr.
Kilpatrick	.	.	.	Colquhoun.
King	.	.	.	MacGregor.
Kinnell	.	.	.	MacDonald.
Kinnieson	.	.	.	MacFarlane.
Kirkpartick	.	.	.	Colquhoun.
Lachlan	.	.	.	MacLachlan.
Lamb	.	.	.	Lamont.
Lambie	.	.	.	Do.
Lammie	.	.	.	Do.
Lamond	.	.	.	Do.
Lamondson	.	.	.	Do.
Lamont	.	.	.	Lamont.
Landers	.	.	.	Do.
Lang	.	.	.	Leslie.
Lauder	.	.	.	Lauder.
Lean	.	.	.	Maclean.
Leckie	.	.	.	MacGregor.

Sept.	Clan.
Lecky	MacGregor.
Lees	Macpherson.
Lemond . . .	Lamont.
Lennie or Lenny .	Buchanan.
Lennox . . .	MacFarlane, Stewart (Royal).
Leslie	Leslie.
Lewis	MacLeod of Lewis.
Leys	Farquharson.
Limond, Limont .	Lamont.
Lindsay . . .	Lindsay.
Linklater . . .	Sinclair.
Livingston . . .	Stewart of Appin.
Livingstone . .	Do.
Lobban . . .	Maclennan.
Logan	Do.
Loudoun . . .	Campbell of Loudoun.
Love	Mackinnon.
Lucas	Lamont.
Luke	Do.
Lyon	Farquharson, Lamont.
Mac a' Challies .	MacDonald.
Macachounich .	Colquhoun.
MacAdam . .	MacGregor.
MacAdie . . .	Ferguson.
MacAindra . .	MacFarlane.
MacAlaster . .	MacAlister.
Macaldonach .	Buchanan.
Macalduie . .	Lamont.
MacAlester . .	MacAlister.
MacAlister . .	Do.
MacAllan . . .	MacDonald of Clanranald, MacFarlane.
MacAllaster . .	MacAlister.
MacAllister . .	Do.
MacAlpin . . .	MacAlpine.
MacAlpine . .	Do.
Macandeoir . .	Buchanan, Macnab.
MacAndrew . .	Mackintosh.
MacAngus . .	Macinnes.
Macara . . .	MacGregor, Macrae.
Macaree . . .	MacGregor.
MacArthur . .	MacArthur.
MacAskill . .	MacLeod of Lewis.
MacAslan . .	Buchanan.

Sept.			Clan.
MacAulay	.	.	MacAulay, MacLeod of Lewis.
MacAuselan	.	.	Buchanan.
MacAuslan	.	.	Do.
MacAusland	.	.	Do.
MacAuslane	.	.	Do.
MacAy	.	.	Mackintosh (Shaw).
MacBain	.	.	MacBean.
MacBaxter	.	.	Macmillan.
MacBean	.	.	MacBean.
MacBeath	.	.	MacBean, MacDonald, Maclean of Duart.
MacBeolain	.	.	MacKenzie.
MacBeth	.	.	MacBean, MacDonald, Maclean of Duart.
MacBheath	.	.	Do. do.
MacBrayne	.	.	MacNaughton.
MacBride	.	.	MacDonald.
MacBrieve	.	.	Morrison.
MacBurie	.	.	MacDonald of Clanranald.
MacCaa	.	.	MacFarlane.
MacCaig	.	.	Farquharson, MacLeod of Harris.
MacCainsh	.	.	Macinnes.
MacCaishe	.	.	MacDonald.
MacCall	.	.	Do.
MacCallum	.	.	MacCallum.
MacCalman	.	.	Buchanan.
MacCalmont	.	.	Do.
MacCamie	.	.	Stuart of Bute.
MacCammon	.	.	Buchanan.
MacCammond	.	.	Do.
MacCansh	.	.	Macinnes.
MacCardney	.	.	Farquharson, Mackintosh.
MacCartair	.	.	Campbell of Strachur (Mac-Arthur).
MacCarter	.	.	Do. do.
MacCash	.	.	MacDonald.
MacCaskill	.	.	MacLeod of Lewis.
MacCaul	.	.	MacDonald.
MacCause	.	.	MacFarlane.
MacCaw	.	.	MacFarlane, Stuart of Bute.
MacCay	.	.	Mackay.
MacCeallaich	.	.	MacDonald.
MacChlerich	.	.	Cameron, Mackintosh, Mac-pherson.
MacChlery	.	.	Do. do.

Sept.			Clan.
MacChoiter	.	.	MacGregor.
MacChruiter	.	.	Buchanan.
MacCloy	.	.	Stuart of Bute.
MacClure	.	.	MacLeod of Harris.
MacClymont	.	.	Lamont.
MacColdrum	.	.	MacDonald.
MacColl	.	.	Do.
MacColman	.	.	Buchanan.
MacComas	.	.	Gunn.
MacCombe	.	.	Mackintosh.
MacCombich	.	.	Stewart of Appin.
MacCombie	.	.	Mackintosh.
MacComie	.	.	Do.
MacConacher	.	.	MacDougall.
MacConachie	.	.	Robertson.
MacConchy	.	.	Mackintosh.
MacCondy	.	.	MacFarlane.
MacConnach	.	.	MacKenzie.
MacConnechy	.	.	Campbell of Inverawe, Robertson.
MacConnell	.	.	MacDonald.
MacConochie	.	.	Campbell of Inverawe, Robertson.
MacCooish	.	.	MacDonald.
MacCook	.	.	MacDonald of Kintyre.
MacCorkill	.	.	Gunn.
MacCorkindale	.	.	MacCorquodale.
MacCorkle	.	.	Gunn.
MacCormack	.	.	Buchanan.
MacCormick	.	.	Maclaine of Lochbuie.
MacCorquodale	.	.	MacCorquodale.
MacCorrie	.	.	Macquarrie.
MacCorry	.	.	Do.
MacCoull	.	.	MacDougall.
MacCowan	.	.	Colquhoun.
MacCrae	.	.	Macrae.
MacCrain	.	.	MacDonald.
MacCraw	.	.	Macrae.
Macreath	.	.	Do.
MacCrie	.	.	Do.
MacCrimmon	.	.	MacLeod of Harris.
MacCuag	.	.	MacDonald of Kintyre.
MacCuaig	.	.	Farquharson, MacLeod of Harris.
MacCuish	.	.	MacDonald.
MacCuithein	.	.	Do.
MacCulloch	.	.	MacDougall, Munro, Ross.
MacCunn	.	.	Macqueen.

Sept.			Clan.
MacCurrach	.	.	Macpherson.
MacCutchen	.	.	MacDonald.
MacCutcheon	.	.	Do.
Macdade	.	.	Davidson.
Macdaid	.	.	Do.
MacDaniell	.	.	MacDonald.
MacDavid	.	.	Davidson.
MacDermid	.	.	Campbell of Argyll.
MacDiarmid	.	.	Do. do.
MacDonachie	.	.	Robertson.
MacDonald (Clan Donald)	.	.	MacDonald.
MacDonald of Ardna-murchan	.	.	MacDonald of Ardnamurchan.
MacDonald of Clanranald	.	.	MacDonald of Clanranald.
MacDonell of Glengarry	.	.	MacDonell of Glengarry.
MacDonell of Keppoch	.	.	MacDonell of Keppoch.
Macdonleavy	.	.	Buchanan.
MacDougall	.	.	MacDougall.
MacDowall	.	.	Do.
MacDowell	.	.	Do.
Macdrain	.	.	MacDonald.
MacDuff	.	.	Wemyss.
MacDuffie	.	.	Macfie.
MacDulothe	.	.	MacDougall.
MacEachan	.	.	MacDonald of Clanranald.
MacEachern	.	.	MacDonald.
MacEachin	.	.	MacDonald of Clanranald.
MacEachran	.	.	MacDonald.
MacEarachar	.	.	Farquharson.
MacElfrish	.	.	MacDonald.
MacElheran	.	.	MacDonald.
MacEoin	.	.	MacFarlane.
Maceol	.	.	MacNaughton.
MacErracher	.	.	MacFarlane.
MacEwen	.	.	MacEwan.
MacFadyen	.	.	Maclaine of Lochbuie.
MacFadzean	.	.	Do. do.
MacFall	.	.	Mackintosh.
MacFarlan	.	.	MacFarlane.
MacFarlane	.	.	Do.
MacFarquhar	.	.	Farquharson.
MacFater	.	.	MacLaren.
MacFeat	.	.	Do.
MacFergus	.	.	Ferguson.
Macfie or Macfee	.	.	Macfie.

Sept.			Clan.
MacGaw	.	.	MacFarlane.
MacGeachie	.	.	MacDonald of Clanranald.
MacGeachin	.	.	Do. do.
MacGeoch	.	.	MacFarlane.
Macghee	.	.	Mackay.
Macghie	.	.	Do.
MacGibbon	.	.	Buchanan of Sallochy, Campbell of Argyll, Graham of Menteith.
MacGilbert	.	.	Buchanan of Sallochy.
MacGilchrist	.	.	MacLachlan, Ogilvie.
MacGilledow	.	.	Lamont.
MacGillegowie	.	.	Do.
MacGillivantic	.	.	MacDonell of Keppoch.
MacGillivoor	.	.	MacGillivray.
MacGillivray	.	.	Do.
MacGillonie	.	.	Cameron.
MacGilp	.	.	MacDonell of Keppoch.
MacGilroy	.	.	Grant of Glenmoriston, MacGillivray.
MacGilvernock	.	.	Graham of Menteith.
MacGilvra	.	.	MacGillivray, Maclaine of Lochbuie.
MacGilvray	.	.	MacGillivray.
Macglashan	.	.	Mackintosh. Stewart of Atholl.
Macglasrich	.	.	MacIvor (Campbell of Argyll), MacDonell of Keppoch.
MacGorrie	.	.	MacDonald, Macquarrie.
MacGorry	.	.	Do. do.
MacGoun	.	.	MacDonald, Macpherson.
MacGowan	.	.	MacDonald, Macpherson.
MacGown	.	.	Do. do.
MacGregor	.	.	MacGregor.
MacGreusich	.	.	Buchanan, MacFarlane.
MacGrory	.	.	MacLaren.
Macgrowther	.	.	MacGregor.
MacGrigor	.	.	Do.
Macgrime	.	.	Graham of Menteith.
Macgruder	.	.	MacGregor.
Macgruer	.	.	Fraser.
Macgruther	.	.	MacGregor.
MacGuaig	.	.	Farquharson.
MacGuaran	.	.	Macquarrie.
MacGuffie	.	.	Macfie.
MacGuire	.	.	Macquarrie.

Sept.			Clan.
Machaffie	.	.	Macfie.
Machardie, Machardy	.	.	Farquharson, Mackintosh.
MacHarold	.	.	Macleod of Harris.
MacHay	.	.	Mackintosh (Shaw).
MacHendrie	.	.	MacNaughton.
MacHendry	.	.	Do.
MacHenry	.	.	MacDonald (MacIan) of Glencoe.
MacHowell	.	.	MacDougall.
MacHugh	.	.	MacDonald.
MacHutchen	.	.	Do.
MacHutcheon	.	.	Do.
MacIan	.	.	Gunn, MacDonald of Ardnamurchan, MacDonald of Glencoe.
Macildowie	.	.	Cameron.
Macilduy	.	.	MacGregor, Maclean of Duart.
Macilleriach	.	.	MacDonald.
Macilreach	.	.	Do.
Macilrevie	.	.	Do.
Macilriach	.	.	Do.
Macilroy	.	.	MacGillivray, Grant of Glenmoriston.
Macilvain	.	.	MacBean.
Macilvora	.	.	Maclaine of Lochbuie.
Macilvrae	.	.	MacGillivray.
Macilvride	.	.	MacDonald.
Macilwhom	.	.	Lamont.
Macilwraith	.	.	MacDonald.
Macilzegowie	.	.	Lamont.
Macimmey	.	.	Fraser.
Macinally	.	.	Buchanan.
Macindeor	.	.	Menzies.
Macindoe	.	.	Buchanan.
Macinnes	.	.	Macinnnes, Innes
Macinroy	.	.	Robertson.
Macinstalker	.	.	MacFarlane.
Macintosh	.	.	Mackintosh.
Macintyre	.	.	Macintyre.
MacIock	.	.	MacFarlane.
MacIsaac	.	.	Campbell of Craignish, MacDonald of Clanranald.
MacIver, MacIvor	.	.	Campbell of Argyll, Robertson of Struan, MacKenzie.
MacJames	.	.	MacFarlane.

Sept.			Clan.
MacKail	.	.	Cameron.
MacKames	.	.	Gunn.
Mackay	.	.	Mackay.
MacKeachan	.	.	MacDonald of Clanranald.
MacKeamish	.	.	Gunn.
MacKean	.	.	Gunn, MacDonald of Ardna-murchan, MacDonald of Glencoe.
Mackechnie	.	.	MacDonald of Clanranald.
Mackee	.	.	Mackay.
Mackeggie	.	.	Mackintosh.
MacKeith	.	.	Macpherson.
MacKellachie	.	.	MacDonald.
MacKellaig	.	.	Do.
MacKellaigh	.	.	Do.
MacKellar	.	.	Campbell of Argyll.
MacKelloch	.	.	MacDonald.
MacKendrick	.	.	MacNaughton.
MacKenrick	.	.	Do.
MacKenzie	.	.	MacKenzie.
MacKeochan	.	.	MacDonald of Clanranald.
MacKerchar	.	.	Farquharson.
MacKerlich	.	.	MacKenzie.
MacKerrachar	.	.	Farquharson.
MacKerras	.	.	Ferguson.
MacKersey	.	.	Do.
MacKessock	.	.	Campbell of Craignish, Mac-Donald of Clanranald.
MacKichan	.	.	MacDonald of Clanranald, MacDougall.
Mackie	.	.	Mackay.
MacKillican	.	.	Mackintosh.
MacKillop	.	.	MacDonell of Keppoch.
MacKim	.	.	Fraser.
MacKimmie	.	.	Do.
Mackindlay	.	.	Farquharson.
Mackinlay	.	.	Mackinlay.
Mackinley	.	.	Buchanan.
MacKinnell	.	.	MacDonald.
Mackinney	.	.	Mackinnon.
Mackinning	.	.	Do.
Mackinnon	.	.	Do.
Mackintosh	.	.	Mackintosh.
Mackinven	.	.	Mackinnon.
MacKirdy	.	.	Stuart of Bute.

Sept.			*Clan.*
MacKissock	.	.	Campbell of Craignish, Mac-Donald of Clanranald.
Macknight	.	.	MacNaughton.
MacLachlan	.	.	MacLachlan.
Maclae	.	.	Stewart of Appin.
Maclagan	.	.	Robertson.
MacLaghlan	.	.	MacLachlan.
Maclaine	.	.	Maclaine of Lochbuie.
MacLairish	.	.	MacDonald.
MacLamond	.	.	Lamont.
MacLardie, MacLardy	.	.	MacDonald.
MacLaren	.	.	MacLaren.
MacLarty	.	.	MacDonald.
MacLauchlan	.	.	MacLachlan.
MacLaughlan	.	.	Do.
MacLaurin	.	.	MacLaren.
MacLaverty	.	.	MacDonald.
Maclay	.	.	Stewart of Appin.
Maclea, Macleay	.	.	Livingstone, Stewart.
Maclean	.	.	Maclean.
MacLeish	.	.	Macpherson.
MacLeister	.	.	MacGregor.
MacLellan	.	.	MacDonald.
Maclennan	.	.	Maclennan.
MacLeod of Harris	.	.	MacLeod of Harris.
MacLeod of Lewes	.	.	MacLeod of Lewes.
MacLergain	.	.	Maclean.
Maclerie	.	.	Cameron, Mackintosh, Mac-pherson.
MacLeverty	.	.	MacDonald.
MacLewis	.	.	MacLeod of Lewis, Stuart of Bute.
MaLise	.	.	Macpherson.
MacLiver	.	.	Campbell, MacGregor.
MacLucas	.	.	Lamont, MacDougall.
MacLugash	.	.	MacDougall.
MacLulich	.	.	MacDougall, Munro, Ross.
MacLymont	.	.	Lamont.
MacMartin	.	.	Cameron.
MacMaster	.	.	Buchanan, Macinnes.
MacMath	.	.	Matheson.
MacMaurice	.	.	Buchanan.
MacMenzies	.	.	Menzies.
MacMichael	.	.	Stewart of Appin, Stewart of Galloway.
Macmillan	.	.	Macmillan.

Sept.			*Clan.*
MacMinn	.	.	Menzies.
MacMonies	.	.	Do.
MacMorran	.	.	Mackinnon.
MacMurchie	.	.	Buchanan, MacDonald, MacKenzie.
MacMurchy	.	.	Do. do.
MacMurdo	.	.	MacDonald, Macpherson.
MacMurdoch	.	.	Do. do.
MacMurray	.	.	Murray.
MacMurrich	.	.	MacDonald of Clanranald, Macpherson.
MacMutrie	.	.	Stuart of Bute.
Macnab	.	.	Macnab.
MacNachdan	.	.	MacNaughton.
MacNachton	.	.	Do.
MacNaghten	.	.	Do.
MacNair	.	.	MacFarlane, MacNaughton.
MacNauchton	.	.	MacNaughton.
MacNaughtan	.	.	Do.
MacNaughton	.	.	Do.
MacNayer	.	.	Do.
MacNeal of Barra		.	MacNeil of Barra.
MacNeal of Gigha		.	McNeill of Gigha.
MacNee	.	.	MacGregor.
MacNeil of Barra	.	.	MacNeil of Barra.
MacNeil, McNeil of Gigha		.	McNeill of Gigha.
MacNeilage	.	.	MacNeil.
MacNeiledge	.	.	Do.
MacNeish	.	.	MacGregor.
MacNelly	.	.	MacNeil.
MacNeur	.	.	MacFarlane.
MacNichol	.	.	Campbell of Argyll.
MacNicol	.	.	MacNicol.
MacNider	.	.	MacFarlane.
MacNie	.	.	MacGregor.
MacNiel of Barra	.	.	MacNiel of Barra.
MacNish	.	.	MacGregor.
MacNiter	.	.	MacFarlane.
MacNiven	.	.	Cumin, Mackintosh, MacNaughton.
MacNuir	.	.	MacNaughton.
MacNuyer	.	.	Buchanan, MacNaughton, MacFarlane.
MacOmie	.	.	Mackintosh.

Sept.			Clan.
MacOmish	.	.	Gunn.
MacOnie	.	.	Cameron.
MacOran	.	.	Campbell of Melfort.
MacO'Shannaig	.	.	MacDonald of Kintyre.
Macoul	.	.	MacDougall.
MacOurlic	.	.	Cameron.
MacOwen	.	.	Campbell of Argyll.
Macowl	.	.	MacDougall.
MacPatrick	.	.	Lamont, MacLaren.
MacPeter	.	.	MacGregor.
MacPhail	.	.	Clan Chattan.
MacPhater	.	.	MacLaren.
MacPhedron	.	.	MacAulay.
Macphee	.	.	Macfie.
MacPheidiran	.	.	MacAulay.
Macpherson	.	.	Macpherson.
MacPhilip	.	.	MacDonell of Keppoch.
MacPhorich	.	.	Lamont.
MacPhun	.	.	Matheson.
Macquaire	.	.	Macquarrie.
Macquarrie	.	.	Do.
Macqueen	.	.	Macqueen.
Macquey	.	.	Mackay.
Macquhirr	.	.	Macquarrie.
Macquire	.	.	Do.
MacQuistan	.	.	MacDonald.
MacQuisten	.	.	Do.
Macquoid	.	.	Mackay.
Macra	.	.	Macrae.
Macrach	.	.	Do.
Macrae	.	.	Do.
Macrailt	.	.	MacLeod of Harris.
MacRaith	.	.	Macrae, Macilwraith, Mac-Donald.
MacRankin	.	.	Maclean of Coll.
MacRath	.	.	Macrae.
Macritchie	.	.	Mackintosh.
MacRob	.	.	Gunn, MacFarlane, Innes.
MacRobb	.	.	MacFarlane.
MacRobbie	.	.	Robertson.
MacRobert	.	.	Do.
MacRobie	.	.	Do.
MacRorie	.	.	MacDonald.
MacRory	.	.	MacDonald, MacLaren.
MacRuer	.	.	MacDonald.

Sept.			Clan.
MacRurie	.	.	MacDonald.
MacRury	.	.	Do.
MacShannachan	.	.	Do.
MacShimes	.	.	Fraser.
MacSimon	.	.	Do.
MacSorley	.	.	Cameron, MacDonald, Lamont.
MacSporran	.	.	Macdonald.
MacSuain	.	.	Macqueen.
MacSwan	.	.	Macqueen, MacDonald.
MacSween	.	.	Macqueen.
MacSwen	.	.	Do.
MacSwyde	.	.	Do.
MacSymon	.	.	Fraser.
MacTaggart	.	.	Ross.
MacTary	.	.	Innes.
MacTause	.	.	Campbell of Argyll.
MacTavish	.	.	MacTavish.
MacTear	.	.	Ross, Macintyre.
MacThomas	.	.	Campbell of Argyll, Mackintosh.
MacTier	.	.	Ross.
MacTire	.	.	Do.
MacUlric	.	.	Cameron.
MacUre	.	.	Campbell of Argyll.
Macvail	.	.	Cameron, Mackay, Mackintosh.
MacVanish	.	.	MacKenzie.
MacVarish	.	.	MacDonald of Clanranald.
MacVeagh	.	.	Maclean of Duart.
MacVean	.	.	MacBean.
MacVey	.	.	Maclean of Duart.
MacVicar	.	.	Campbell, MacNaughton.
MacVinish	.	.	MacKenzie.
MacVurie	.	.	MacDonald of Clanranald.
MacVurrich	.	.	MacDonald of Clanrana, Macpherson.
MacWalrick	.	.	Cameron.
MacWalter	.	.	MacFarlane.
MacWattie	.	.	Buchanan of Leny.
MacWhannell	.	.	MacDonald.
MacWhirr	.	.	Macquarrie.
MacWhirter	.	.	Buchanan.
MacWilliam	.	.	Gunn, MacFarlane.
Macgrath	.	.	Macrae.
Malcolm	.	.	Malcolm.
Malcolmson	.	.	MacLeod of Raasay.
Malloch	.	.	MacGregor.

Sept.	Clan.
Manson	Gunn.
Marnoch	Innes.
Martin	Cameron, MacDonald.
Masterson	Buchanan.
Matheson	Matheson.
Mathie, Mathieson	Do.
Mavor	Innes.
Maxwell	Maxwell.
May	MacDonald.
Means	Menzies.
Meikleham	Lamont.
Mein or Meine	Menzies.
Mengues, Mennie	Do.
Menteith	Graham of Menteith.
Menzies	Menzies.
Meyners	Do.
Michie	Forbes.
Middleton	Innes.
Mill, Milne	Gordon, Innes, Ogilvie.
Miller	MacFarlane.
Minn, Minnus	Menzies.
Mitchell	Innes.
Monach	MacFarlane.
Monroe	Munro.
Monteith	Graham of Menteith.
Montgomerie	Montgomerie.
Monzie	Menzies.
Moray	Murray.
More	Leslie.
Morgan	Mackay.
Morison	Morrison.
Morrison	Do.
Mowat	Sutherland.
Munro, Munroe	Munro.
Murchie	Buchanan, MacDonald, MacKenzie.
Murchison	Buchanan, MacDonald, MacKenzie.
Murdoch	MacDonald, Macpherson.
Murdoson	Do. do.
Murray of Atholl	Murray of Atholl.
Murray of Tullibardine	Murray of Tullibardine.
Napier	MacFarlane.
Neal	MacNeil.

Sept.	*Clan.*
Neil or Neill	MacNeil.
Neilson	Mackay.
Neish	MacGregor.
Nelson	Gunn.
Nicholl	Nicolson.
Nicholson	Do.
Nicol or Nicoll	Do.
Nicolson	Do.
Nish	MacGregor.
Niven	Cumin, Mackintosh, Mac-Naughton.
Noble	Mackintosh.
Norman	MacLeod of Harris.
O'Drain	MacDonald.
Ogilvie	Ogilvie.
Ogilvy	Do.
Oliphant	Sutherland.
O'May	MacDonald.
O'Shaig	Do.
O'Shannachan	Do.
O'Shannaig	Do.
Parlane	MacFarlane.
Paterson	MacLaren.
Patrick	Lamont.
Paul	Cameron, Mackintosh, Mackay.
Peter	MacGregor.
Philipson	MacDonell of Keppoch.
Pitullich	MacDonald.
Polson	Mackay.
Purcell	MacDonald.
Rae	Macrae.
Ramsay	Ramsay.
Rankin	Maclean of Coll.
Rattray	Rattray.
Reid	Robertson of Strathloch.
Reidfuird	Innes.
Reoch	Farquharson, MacDonald.
Revie	MacDonald.
Riach	Farquharson, MacDonald.
Risk	Buchanan.
Ritchie	Mackintosh.
Robb	MacFarlane.

Sept.			Clan.
Robertson	.	.	Robertson.
Robison	.	.	Gunn.
Rob Roy	.	.	MacGregor.
Robson	.	.	Gunn.
Rollo	.	.	Rollo.
Ronald	.	.	MacDonell of Keppoch.
Ronaldson	.	.	Do.
Rorison	.	.	MacDonald.
Rose	.	.	Rose.
Ross	.	.	Ross.
Roy	.	.	Robertson.
Ruskin	.	.	MacCalman (Buchanan).
Russell	.	.	Cumin.
Rutherford	.	.	Home.
Ruthven	.	.	Ruthven.
Sanderson	.	.	MacDonell of Glengarry.
Sandison	.	.	Gunn.
Scott	.	.	Scott.
Seton	.	.	Seton.
Shannon	.	.	MacDonald.
Shaw	.	.	Mackintosh.
Sim or Sime	.	.	Fraser.
Simon	.	.	Do.
Simpson	.	.	Do.
Sinclair	.	.	Sinclair.
Skene	.	.	Skene, Robertson.
Small	.	.	Murray.
Smith	.	.	Gow, Macpherson, **Clan Chattan.**
Sorley	.	.	Cameron, MacDonald, **Lamont.**
Spalding	.	.	Murray.
Spence, Spens	.	.	MacDuff.
Spittal or Spittel	.	.	Buchanan.
Sporran	.	.	MacDonald.
Stalker	.	.	MacFarlane.
Stark	.	.	Robertson.
Steuart	.	.	Stewart.
Stewart of Appin	.	.	Stewart of Appin.
Stewart of Atholl	.	.	Stewart of Atholl.
Stewart of Galloway	.	.	Stewart of Galloway.
Stewart, Royal	.	.	Stewart.
Stuart	.	.	Do.
Stuart of Bute	.	.	Stuart of Bute.
Sutherland	.	.	Sutherland.
Swan	.	.	Macqueen.

Sept.			Clan.
Swanson	.	.	Gunn.
Syme, Symon	.	.	Fraser.
Taggart	.	.	Ross.
Tarrill	.	.	Mackintosh.
Tawesson	.	.	Campbell of Argyll.
Tawse	.	.	Farquharson.
Taylor	.	.	Cameron.
Thain	.	.	Innes.
Thomas	.	.	Campbell, Mackintosh.
Thomason	.	.	Campbell, MacFarlane, Mackintosh.
Thompson	.	.	Campbell of Argyll.
Thomson	.	.	Campbell, Mackintosh.
Todd	.	.	Gordon.
Tolmie	.	.	MacLeod of Raasay.
Tonnochy	.	.	Robertson.
Tosh, Toshach	.	.	Mackintosh.
Toward, Towart	.	.	Lamont.
Train	.	.	MacDonald.
Turner	.	.	Lamont.
Tweedie	.	.	Fraser.
Tyre	.	.	Macintyre.
Ure	.	.	Campbell of Argyll.
Urquhart	.	.	Urquhart.
Vass	.	.	Munro, Ross.
Wallace	.	.	Wallace.
Wallis	.	.	Do.
Warnebald	.	.	Cunningham.
Wass	.	.	Munro, Ross.
Watson	.	.	Buchanan.
Watt	.	.	Do.
Weaver	.	.	MacFarlane.
Weir	.	.	MacNaughton, MacFarlane.
Wemyss	.	.	MacDuff.
Whannell	.	.	MacDonald.
Wharrie	.	.	Macquarrie.
White or Whyte	.	.	MacGregor, Lamont.
Williamson	.	.	Gunn, Mackay.
Wilson	.	.	Gunn, Innes.
Wright	.	.	Macintyre.
Yuill	.	.	**Buchanan.**
Yule	.	.	Do.

Much discussion rages over the antiquity of tartans, and which are " authentic." Some are ancient, others comparatively—and some quite—modern. Their " authenticity " is not a question of *age*, but whether they *are* the design which the Chief, as Representative of the Clan, uses, or approves, as the Clan Tartan. Excepting the " district," " Caledonia " and " Jacobite " tartans, no one should wear a tartan to which he is not by name or descent entitled. To do so is foolish and ill-mannered, invites scorn, and is contrary to the whole principle of the Clan System. Nor does one " select " tartans from this or that " line " of ancestors.

WHAT TARTAN CAN I WEAR?

The vital question is, " To which Clan do I *belong*? " (1) You " belong " to the clan of which you bear the surname or a sept name. (2) You have no real right to wear your mother's tartan *unless* you have taken her name. (3) You cannot belong to several clans at once. (4) Adherents (*cliathe*) of non-clan names are, as followers, sometimes allowed to wear the tartan (usually hunting sett if any) and to become associate-members (at higher subscription) of a clan society.

For list of printed Clan and Family Histories, consult Margaret Stuart, *Scottish Family History*, 1928. Genealogies of Chiefs and Chieftains are recorded, either with their arms in *Lyon Register*, or in the *Register of Genealogies*, kept by the Lord Lyon King of Arms, who exercises the Celtic jurisdiction of the High Sennachie of Scotland. Government search fee £1 1s. ($3). (Casual inquiries about tartans and septs are not entertained.) Pedigrees of most Chiefs and many Chieftains are published in *Burke's Peerage* and *Burke's Landed Gentry*, obtainable at most libraries.

THE SCOTTISH CLAN SYSTEM

A CLAN is a social group consisting of an aggregate of distinct branch-families actually descended from, or accepting themselves as descendants of a common ancestor, and which group has been received, in the person of its " Representer," by the Crown, either through a " Charter of Chieftainry " (such as those issued by David II.), or through the King's " Supreme Officer of Honour " (the Lord Lyon) as an " Honourable community " in the *communitas Regni Scotiae*. If such a group comprehends only families of one surname (the chief's), it is, or may be called a " Name," but (as the Very Rev. L. Maclean Watt has said) " Clan and Family mean exactly the same thing." The word *clan* simply means " children," so the community-idea is necessarily based on an Hereditary Parent—the Chief, but it also envisages a *home*—the *duthus*.

The clan has been described as " a mixture of tribal tradition clustering round the actual landholder of the soil " (I. P. Grant, *Lordship of the Isles*, 327). Feudalism " became an integral part of the Clan System " (*Clans, Septs and Regiments of the Scottish Highlands*, 3rd ed., p. xix), because in its *true* sense " feudalism " (a much misunderstood word) meant the " *organisation of the family upon the land*," that is, in relation to its native district, the Celtic title to which was descent from the patriarch who " first raised smoke and boiled water on that land." Such tenure was *allodial, i.e.* " under God " (as the King's sovereignty still is) ; though, in building up a tribal-kingdom, the *allods* (a tenure still subsisting in the *Udal* lands of Orkney) were by contract converted into perpetual *feu*-tenure, under the *Ard-righ* and chiefs as fatherly Representers. The King and the " Seven Earls " were held to represent the " seven sons of Cruithne the Pict "—the whole kingdom being thus a national clan-concept. A special element " mingled from the first in the feudality of Scotland and has left its indelible impress on the manners and habits of thought of the country. The blood of the highest nobles . . . was flowing in that of the workers, at no remote interval. This was a subject of pride " (*Lives of the Lindsays*, 117). The " natural affinity between the national character of the people and their form of Government and social organisation made the (Scottish) feudal system a truly popular one " (I.F. Grant, *Social and Economic Development of Scotland*, 198). Thus " the clan system was feudal in the strictly historical sense " (A. Mure Mackenzie, *History of Scotland*, 41). But feudalism

51

in its *true* and historical sense simply means " the organisation of the Family, and in relation to the Land " (*Proc. of Society of Antiquaries of Scotland*, Vol. 77, pp. 164–174). The Clan was aristocratic and pastoral—the most broad-based aristocracy in the world. The Clan System represented the ideal union of People and Land, their native " clan-countries," in organized family-groups, forming a colourful and vigorously healthy civilisation, in which stately demeanour, pride of ancestry, and graceful manners were shared by all (D. Stewart of Garth, *Sketches of the Highlanders*, 1825, pp. 50, 60, 100).

The *Tighern* (" house-lord "—Scots *thane*), or *Ceantighe* (each meaning " head of the house ") is the hereditary " Representer of the Family " in the tribal sense, comprehending its whole " following," whether " be pretence of blude or place of their dwelling " (*Acts of Parliament of Scotland*, iv. 40) ; whilst the *duthus* is the hereditary property of the successive chief or chieftain. The Clan, and a Family, were themselves regarded as an " heritable " (and noble) subject ; so that this, with the arms and banner, could descend, even if, by misfortune, the *duthus* were lost and the clan became landless. The office of Chief, *i.e.* representer of the founder and of his *communitas* (family), passed heritably (by nomination or by law) from chieftain to chieftain, who ruled with advice of a family/clan Council, which in the formalised feudal organisation became the Baron-Court—the parliament of the little family-state, an aristo-democratic system, struck at, but *not* " abolished," by the Heritable Jurisdictions Act, 1748, which, with the proscription of Highland dress repealed 1782), was meant to destroy the clan system. The *Ard-Righ*/sovereign is in the tribal sense " father of all the fathers " (chiefs, lairds, and peers), the main branches of the " national family," under whom the chieftain/*tighern* are the " parents " of the smaller branches springing from their own " houses," and sub-divided into *gilfine* in each *duthus*. The whole system is thus a family-organisation rising pyramid-wise from the cottar-house, ha'hoose and castle to the royal palace ; but throughout it is the picturesque and healthy " family," rooted in the land ; and this explains why, in Scotland, there is such pride in rank and titles, but no class division and distinction (Innes of Learney, *Scots Heraldry*, pp. 1–4).

Those who think of a nation as a "Family" too often forget that the social success of the Clan-System has lain in making this " family " character human and real (*a*) The great-family has to be divided into branches and sub-branches. (*b*) Though governed with family and branch " councils," the " representation " must be biologically hereditary, or the *link of nature* is lost. (A " clan "—the very word means " children "—with an

' elected chief " would resemble not a family but an orphan-
age ! If an election becomes essential, as when the heirs of the
chiefs cannot be traced, and the last has nominated no *tanist*, an
electee becomes the subject of a *heritable* confirmation of " the
arms "). (*c*) The seat of the chiefs forms the " hearth of the
race," over which the arms of the *eponymus* are emblazoned—
insignia, not of " class," but of family-representership. (Lord
Justice-Clerk Aitchison recently emphasised that " the inheritor
of the family estate " (the *duthus*) is " the Representer of the
Family " ; and in 1680 Lord Advocate Sir George Mackenzie
laid down of the armorial " chief " that " so we call the
Representative of the Family," and that in Gaelic, " the Representative of the Family is called the Head of the Clan," thus
emphasising the tribal character of Scotland's whole social
system. *Tartans of the Clans and Families of Scotland*, p. 26).
The chief feels responsible not only for his own destiny, but
also for that of all his clan, who in times of difficulty unite in
helping him. In the words of Lord Lovat, " There is no earthly
thing I put in balance with my kindred . . . my guard, my glory,
and honour." All thus join in preserving the traditions and
honour of the Clan.

Clan Societies have existed since the seventeenth century.
They provide invaluable machinery for a clan-fund, repository
for records and treasures, and virtually form the Civil Service
of the clan.

Until about the eighteenth century, most people in the Highlands used " genealogical " surnames, *e.g.* " Alastair mac-
Tearlach macAngus macIan Dhu," only the chief using the
" Clan-name." When surnames became fixed, such a clansman
might become a " MacTearlach," a " MacAngus," a " MacIan,"
or a " MacIndoe." From old records are found evidence of
such " names " being dependers on distinct chiefs or chieftains,
and thus arise many of the Clan-Septs of surnames distinct from
that of the Clan itself.

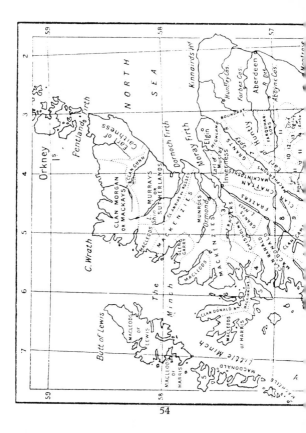

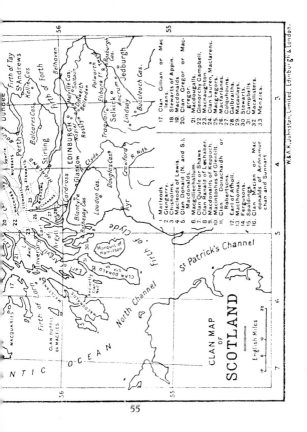

CLAN MAP
OF
SCOTLAND

English Miles

17. Clan Gillian or Mac Ieans
18. Stewarts of Appin.
19. Macdonalds
20. Clan Gregor or Mac- Gregor.
21. Macdougalls.
22. Glenorchy Campbell.
23. Macnaughton.
24. Macfarlane, Maclarens.
25. Macgregors.
26. Macfarlanes.
27. Colquhouns.
28. Galbraiths.
29. Buchanan.
30. Stewarts.
31. Campbells.
32. Macallisters.
33. Menzies.

1. Macleods
2. Glengarry.
3. Chisholms.
4. Macleods of Lewis
5. Clan Donald (N. and S.)
   Macdonalds.
6. Macgillechallum.
7. Clan Quhele or Shaws
8. Clan Ranald of Lochaber.
9. Macdonalds of Keppoch.
10. Macintoshes of Glentilt.
11. Clan Donachaidh or Robertsons.
12. Earl of Atholl.
13. Macthomas.
14. Fergusons.
15. Spaldings.
16. Clan Macian or Mac- donald of Ardnamurchan and Sunart.

W.& A.K.Johnston, Limited. Edinburgh & London.

THE CLAN ANDERSON

(MacAndrew)

This surname means literally the son of Andrew, but as held by families of Lowland origin, denotes, it has been suggested, a "servant of St. Andrew," the patron saint of Scotland. The name is common all over the Lowlands, as well as in Aberdeenshire.

The Gaelic equivalent of Anderson is "Mac Aindrea," son of Andrew, or "Gilleaindrais"—Gillanders, or St. Andrew's gille, so that these Andersons are probably an off-shoot of Clan Aindreas (Ross). These MacAndrews are regarded as a sept of Clan Chattan. Kinrara (1676) after recording the association of the MacQueens, or Clan Revan, says :— "And sick-like Donald MacGillandrish, of whom the Clan Andrish are named, came out of Muidart, with Mora Macdonald, Lady Mackintosh" (Clan Ranald's daughter).

The descendants of MacGillandrish settled in Connage of Petty. In course of time the name was anglicised as MacAndrew. Gillanders is another variation of the original Gaelic.

The most prominent branches of Clan Anderson have been the Andersons of Dowhill, traced from 1540, the Andersons of Wester Ardbreck, in Banffshire, and the Andersons, lairds of Candacraig in Strathdon for ten generations prior to 1865. Arms were awarded in the 16th century to "Anderson of that Ilk" but this family has not been identified. No place "Anderson" ever existed and what the registration implies is that one of the Lindsay Lord Lyons, in the exercise of the Crown's armorial prerogative vested in the Lyon's Office, "received and numbered" one of the Anderson chieftains as representer of the "clan"—as henceforth an "honourable community" whereof the successive heirs of that house would be received in public ceremonial as Representers of the race or clan of Anderson.

1 ANDERSON

BRODIE OF BRODIE

Badge :—Periwinkle.

THIS name is from the local place-name Brodie, Gaelic, *brothach*. The old writings of the family were mostly carried away or destroyed when Lord Lewis Gordon, afterwards (3rd) Marquis of Huntly, burnt Brodie House in 1645. From Malcolm, Thane of Brodie, living *temp.* King Alexander III. descended Alexander Brodie of Brodie, styled Lord Brodie as a senator of the College of Justice, born 1617, whose son and successor, James Brodie of Brodie, born 1637, married in 1659 Lady Mary Ker, daughter of William, 3rd Earl of Lothian. Leaving nine daughters but no son, he was succeeded under settlement by his cousin, George Brodie, son of Joseph Brodie of Aslisk, and grandson of David Brodie of Brodie, brother of Lord Brodie. In 1692 he married Emily, fifth daughter of his predecessor. He died in 1716, leaving three sons and two daughters. James Brodie, the elder son and heir, died young (1720), and was succeeded by his brother, Alexander, born 1697. He was appointed Lord Lyon of Scotland 1727, and died 1754. By his wife, Mary Sleigh, he had a son, Alexander, his heir, and one daughter, Emilia. Alexander Brodie of Brodie, born 1741, died in 1750, and was succeeded by his second cousin, James Brodie, son of James, Brodie of Spynie. This gentleman, Lord-Lieutenant of the county of Nairn, was born, 1744, and married Lady Margaret Duff, youngest daughter of William, 1st Earl of Fife. He died in 1824, leaving two sons and three daughters. Their son, James, was drowned in his father's lifetime, leaving two sons and five daughters. Their eldest son, William Brodie of Brodie, in Morayshire, Lieutenant of Nairnshire, was born in 1799, succeeded his grandfather in January 1824, married in 1838 Elizabeth, third daughter of the late Colonel Hugh Bailie of Red Castle, M.P., and had issue—Hugh Fife Ashley Brodie of Brodie, R.A., born September 1840 and died 1869. His son, Ian Brodie of Brodie, D.S.O., born 1868, Lord-Lieutenant for Nairnshire, died 1943, and was succeeded by his son, the present Chief, Montagu Ninian Brodie of Brodie, whose seat is Brodie Castle. The other branches of this clan are Brodie of Lethen, and Brodie of Eastbourne, Sussex, and a Brodie was made a Baronet in 1834.

2 BRODIE, DRESS

THE HOUSE OF BRUCE

Badge :—Rosemary.

OUR patriot King, Robert the Bruce, belonged to a Norman family, which in the person of Robert de Bruis came to England with the Conqueror in 1066. He received Skelton in Yorkshire, and his son, Robert, an associate of David I. of Scotland, obtained the Lordship of Annandale. At the battle of the Standard (1138) Robert Bruce fought on the English side ; and his son, Robert, 2nd of Annandale, under David, and was taken prisoner, it is said, by his own father. He had two sons, Robert who died before 1191 and William the eventual heir, who died 1215. His son, Robert, 5th Lord, died 1245, having married Isabella of Huntingdon, gread-granddaughter of King David I. Their son, Robert de Bruce, was in 1255 one of the Regents of Scotland, and guardian of Alexander III. In 1290 he claimed the Crown of Scotland, as nearest heir of Alexander III. and also alleged a verbal nomination. King Edward I., having been asked to preside in a Centumviral Court-Tribal, with 104 other " tryours," and having considered the Report of the 80 Scottish " tryours," the Court adjudged the Kingdom of Scotland to Baliol as heir, according to the Scots law of succession, of Margaret, Lady of Scotland (the Maid of Norway). Bruce died in 1295, aged 85. His eldest son, Robert de Bruce, was born in 1245, married Margaret, Countess of Carrick, and died in 1304. His eldest son, Robert the Bruce, was born 11 July 1274. Baliol having disgraced himself and abdicated, The Bruce asserted his claim to the Scottish Crown and was crowned at Scone, 27 March 1306. After many vicissitudes, the power of King Robert I. was finally cemented by his splendid and decisive victory at Bannockburn, 1314. He died at Cardross, Dumbartonshire, 7 June 1329, and was interred in the Abbey Church of Dunfermline.

The Earls of Elgin, descended from Bruce of Clackmannan, who sprang from a cousin of King Robert's, are now acknowledged chiefs of the family. Andrew, 11th Earl, is the present chief. His seat is Broomhall in Fife. The baronial tower of Clackmannan still stands, and is an interesting example of Scots architecture.

3 BRUCE

THE CLAN BUCHANAN

War Cry :—" Clar Innis " (An island in Loch Lomond).
Badge :—Dearc bhraoileag (Bilberry) or Darag (Oak).

ABOUT the middle of the thirteenth century, Gilbert, seneschal to the Earl of Lennox, obtained from him a part of the lands of Buchanan in Stirlingshire and took his name from them. An ecclesiastical origin is claimed for the surname, as in Gaelic a Buchanan is known as *Mac-a'-Chanonaich*—the Son of the Canon—and the place-name Buchanan (*Both-chanain*) really means the canon's seat.

Donald, 6th Earl of Lennox, renewed to Maurice of Buchanan the grant conferred by a former earl on his ancestor, and the King granted a charter of confirmation to his successor of the same name.

Through marriage with a daughter of Menteith of Ruskie, his son, Walter of Buchanan, became connected with the Royal House. The latter married the sole heiress of the ancient family of Leny. Their eldest son, Sir Alexander, distinguished himself as a soldier, and was slain in the battle of Verneuil in 1424. His second brother, Walter, succeeded to Buchanan, and his third to Leny.

Walter married Isabel, Countess of Lennox. Their eldest son, Patrick, married the heiress of Killearn and Auchreoch.

Patrick's son, Walter, married a daughter of Lord Graham. Patrick, who fell at Flodden, by his wife, a daughter of Argyll, left two sons—George, Sheriff of Dumbarton in 1561, and Walter, the founder of the House of Spittal.

By Margaret Edmondston of Duntreath, he had John, his heir, and by his second wife, Janet Cunninghame of Craigends, William, founder of the now extinct line of Auchmar.

The principal line became extinct early in the eighteenth century ; and though in 1878 Francis Hamilton Buchanan of Leny established his claim as Chief, his grandson, J. H. Buchanan of Leny, died in 1919 without issue. Since then the chiefship has been dormant.

The Buchanan family lands are now possessed by the Duke of Montrose. There is a Buchanan Society in Glasgow, which holds Clar-inch, the island in Loch Lomond from which the slogan is derived.

4 BUCHANAN

THE CLAN CAMERON

War Cry :—" Chlanna nan con thigibh a so 's gheibh sibh feòil "
("Sons of the hounds come here and get flesh").
Badge :—Darag (Oak) or Dearca fithich (Crowberry).

THERE are various traditions regarding the early history of Clan
Cameron. Donald Dhu, reckoned 11th Chief, fought at Harlaw
in 1411. He married the heiress of MacMartin of Letterfinlay.
He left two sons—Allan, who succeeded him, and Ewen, who is
generally regarded as the progenitor of the Camerons of Strone.
Allan left two sons, Ewen and John.

Ewen married first a daughter of Celestine of Lochalsh. His
eldest son and heir, Donald, died before his father, between the
years 1536 and 1539. He married secondly, Marjory, daughter
of Lachlan, second son of Malcolm Mackintosh of Mackintosh.
By this lady he had Ewen, the progenitor of the family of Erracht,
and John, progenitor of the Camerons of Kin-Lochiel. Ewen
was succeeded by his grandson, *Eòghan Beag*—Little Ewen—
who was the father of the famous Black Tailor of the Axe.

After Donald and Allan comes the famous Sir Ewen Cameron
of Lochiel, born in 1629. He married first, Mary, daughter of
Sir James MacDonald, 1st Baronet of Sleat, and secondly,
Isabel, daughter of Sir Lachlan Maclean of Duart, and thirdly,
Jane, daughter of Colonel David Barclay (XVII.) of Urie. He
died in 1719, aged ninety.

He was succeeded by his son, John, who married Isabel,
daughter of Campbell of Lochnell, with issue—Donald, who
succeeded, and John of Fassiefern, who died 1747 or 1748.

He was succeeded by Donald, his eldest son, known as " The
Gentle Lochiel," who followed Prince Charlie and suffered with
him. After Culloden he escaped to France, where he died 1748.
He was succeeded in the chiefship by his son, John, who was
succeeded by his brother, Charles. He was succeeded by his
son, Donald, who died 1832. The 25th Chief, Donald's
great-grandson in direct descent, Sir Donald Walter Cameron
of Lochiel, K.T., died in 1951 and was succeeded by his son,
Col. Sir Donald Cameron of Lochiel, K.T.

There is an organisation called " The Clan Cameron," with
its headquarters in Glasgow.

5 CLAN CAMERON

CAMERON OF LOCHIEL

War Cry :—" Chlanna nan con thigibh a so 's gheibh sibh feòil "
    (" Sons of the hounds come here and get flesh ").
    Badge :—Darag (Oak) or Dearca fithich (Crowberry).

THE original possessions of the Camerons were the portion of
Lochaber lying on the east side of the loch and river of Lochy,
held of the Lord of the Isles as superior. Lochiel and Loch-
arkaig, lying on the west side of these waters, were at an earlier
period granted by the Island Lord to MacDonald of Clan Ranald,
by whose descendants they were for some generations held.

The ancient residence of Lochiel was Tor Castle, which was
erected by Ewen Cameron (XIII.) of Lochiel in the beginning
of the sixteenth century, and it remained the seat of the family
till the time of Sir Ewen (XVII.) of Lochiel, who was born in
1629 and died in 1719. He built a mansion, the old Achnacarry,
which was burned in 1746, when the country was overrun and
wasted after Culloden. Achnacarry was rebuilt early in the
nineteenth century but not completed till 1837.

The MacGillonie Camerons are sometimes regarded as the
oldest family of the clan, but in Scotland the heir-male was not
necessarily the chief, and in 1492 the head of the Camerons of
Lochiel was Captain of Clan Cameron, a title then synonymous
with " Chief." In 1528 the King granted a charter erecting all
his land into the Barony of Lochiel, in which the Captain of the
Clan is for the first time designated as " of Lochiel." Since this
the Chief's title has been " Lochiel " ; and in 1795 Donald
Cameron of Lochiel was recognised as chief of the House of
Lochiel and chief of the clan Cameron, by decree of Lyon Court.

The following is a description of the Arms of the Chief :
Gules, three bars or. *Crest*—a sheaf of five arrows proper, tied
with a band gules. *Motto*—" Unite." On a compartment
below the shield, on which are these words " *Pro Rege et Patria*,"
are placed for *Supporters* two savages wreathed about the heads
and middles with oak branches proper, each holding in his
exterior hand a Lochaber axe of the last.

6 CAMERON OF LOCHIEL

THE CAMPBELLS OF ARGYLL

War Cry :—" Cruachan " (A mountain near Loch Awe).
Badge :—Roid (Wild Myrtle) or Garbhag an t-sléibhe
(Fir Club Moss).

DIARMID O'DUINE is generally regarded as the founder of the
clan *Duibhne*, or Campbells. Colin, *Cailein Mòr*, from whom
the Chief gets his patronymic of *Mac Cailein Mòr* was slain at
Ath-Dearg (Red Ford), in Lorn, 1294. The early titles were *de
Ergadia* and Lords of Lochaw.

Sir Colin Campbell (*Cailein Iongantach*) succeeded his father,
Sir Archibald, who died in 1372. He died in 1413, and was
succeeded by his son, Sir Duncan, who was Lord Campbell
prior to 1427. He died in 1453.

Archibald Roy succeeded his father, and was succeeded by
his son, Colin, who was created Earl of Argyll in 1457. He died
in 1493, and was succeeded by his son, Archibald, 2nd Earl
of Argyll, who fell at Flodden. He was succeeded by his son,
Colin, 3rd Earl of Argyll. Archibald, his son, succeeded him,
He died in 1558, and was succeeded by his son, Archibald, who
died without issue in 1575, and was succeeded by his brother,
Colin, 6th Earl of Argyll. Archibald, 7th Earl, reduced
the MacGregors in 1603. He was succeeded by Archibald, his
son, in 1638 as 8th Earl. He was created Marquis of Argyll
in 1641. He was beheaded in 1661. His estates, after being
forfeited, were restored to his son, Archibald, with the title of
Earl of Argyll. For his part in the Monmouth rebellion he has
beheaded 1685. His son, Archibald, 10th Earl, was created
Duke in 1701. He died in 1703, succeeded by his son, John, 2nd
Duke of Argyll and Duke of Greenwich, died 1743. His brother,
Archibald, 3rd Duke, who died 1761, was succeeded by his
cousin, General John Campbell of Mamore. He died in 1770,
succeeded by his son, John, 5th Duke, who died 1790. He left
two sons—George, 6th Duke, died 1839 ; and John, 7th Duke,
who died 1847, leaving George, 8th Duke, died 1900. He had
five sons. The eldest son, John, 9th Duke, born 1845, married
Princess Louise in 1871. His nephew, Niall Diarmid, became
10th Duke in 1914 and died 1949. His cousin, Ian, 12th Duke
is the present chief and is Hereditary Master of H.M. Household.
His seat is Inverary Castle.

7 CAMPBELL OF ARGYLL

THE CAMPBELLS OF BREADALBANE

Badge :—Roid (Wild Myrtle) or Garbhag an t-sléibhe
(Fir Club Moss).

AFTER the House of Argyll, the leading family in Clan Campbell is the House of Campbell of Breadalbane, whose ancestor was Black Colin of Glenorchy, second son of Sir Duncan Campbell, Knight of Loch Awe, by his wife, Lady Marjory Stewart. This accounts for the patronymic of the House of Breadalbane—*Mac-Chailein-Mhic-Dhonnachaidh* (son of Colin son of Duncan). In 1432 Sir Colin received from his father the lands of Glenorchy.

He married Margaret Stewart, co-heiress of John, Lord of Lorn. With her he received the third of the lands of Lorn. Sir Colin died in 1473. Sir Duncan Campbell, 7th of Glenorchy, known as " Black Duncan of the Cowl," was created a Baronet in 1625.

The 1st Earl was Sir John (11th Laird and 5th Bt.), known as *Iain Glas.* He was born in 1635, and was created Earl of Caithness in 1677, having married the widow of the 6th Earl ; but Sinclair of Keiss establishing his claim to that peerage, Glenorchy was in 1681 created Earl of Breadalbane. On the death of his grandson, John, 3rd Earl, the succession passed to John, 4th Earl, the lineal descendant of Colin of Mocastle, second son of Robert, 3rd Bt. of Glenorchy. He was created in 1806 Baron Breadalbane of Taymouth. John, 2nd Marquis and 5th Earl, succeeded his father in 1834. He died without issue in 1862, when the Marquisate of Breadalbane became extinct, and he was succeeded in the Scottish dignities by John 6th Earl of Breadalbane. His son Gavin, 7th Earl was re-created Marquis of Breadalbane, 1885. He died without issue, 1922, when the Scottish honours devolved upon his nephew, Iain, 8th Earl, born 1885, died 1923. He was succeeded by a kinsman, Charles, 9th Earl of Breadalbane, whose son is now 10th Earl and 21st chief of the House of Glenorchy.

There is a Clan Campbell Society, with its headquarters in Glasgow.

8 CAMPBELL OF BREADALBANE

THE CLAN CHISHOLM

THE earliest traces of the Chisholms in Scotland are found in the west of Roxburghshire, where the Lairds of Chisholme were successively called " De Chesé," " de Chesèholm," " de Chesholme vel Chesholme." The original Border seat was the Barony of Chisholme, in Roxburghshire. In the fourteenth century Sir Robert de Chisholme came to the Highlands, and became Constable of Urquhart Castle. His son, Alexander, married Margaret, Lady of Erchless, daughter and heiress of Weyland of the Aird. Their son, Thomas, as heir of line became chief of the tribe of the Aird. The Chisholms in the North becoming strong in wealth and followers, severed from the Border house and held independent sway. The North Country Chisholms, or as they are called, the Strathglass Chisholms, six hundred years ago held lands in Forfar, Perth, Aberdeen, Moray, Inverness, Ross, Sutherland, and Caithness shires ; but later their whole estates were in Inverness and Ross shires, and even these are gone. Erchless Castle was the Chief's seat. Sir Robert and his descendants held their lands in the male line till 1884, when the then Chief, James Sutherland, and his son and heir took advantage of the Act of 1848 and barred the entail, in virtue of which they alone obtained possession. Had the entail not been so barred the property would have reverted to James Gooden Chisholm, grandson of Alexander the entailer, through his daughter Mary Chisholm of Chisholm. After the death, unmarried, in 1887, of Roderick, the estates went by trust-disposition to the widow and daughters, and have since been sold. The chief arms and title *Chisholm of Chisholm*, however, have descended through James Gooden Chisholm to Capt. Roderick Chisholm of Chisholm, to whom the Arms were confirmed by Lyon Court in 1938, and his grandson, Alastair Chisholm of Chisholm, is the present Chief of the clan. He resides at Silver Willows, Bury St. Edmunds.

The Chief of the Chisholms is called in Gaelic " *An Siosalach*," and in Scots, " The Chisholm."

9 CHISHOLM

THE CLAN COLQUHOUN

War Cry :—" Cnoc Ealachain."
Badge :—Caltuinn (Hazel).

THE surname of this clan is a territorial one. The first who assumed it was Ingram, the successor of Humphry Kirkpatrick, who is designated in a charter of Luss by Maldwin, Earl of Lennox, to Malcolm, Laird of Luss, confirming John, Laird of Luss, his charter of the lands of Colchoun.

Sir Humphry Colquhoun, 12th Laird of Luss, acquired the Heritable Coronership of Dunbartonshire in 1583. He died without issue, and was succeeded by his brother, Sir Alexander, who fought the battle of Glenfruin with the MacGregors. His son, Sir John, was created a Baronet in 1625. Sir Humphry, 5th Bt. of Luss, married a daughter of Houston of that Ilk, by whom he had only a daughter, Anne, who in 1702 married James Grant of Pluscardine, second son of Grant of that Ilk. Being resolved that the young couple should succeed him in his estate and honours, in 1704 he resigned his baronetcy to the Crown, and obtained a new grant—to himself in lirerent, to his daughter and son-in-law in fee, providing that their heirs should bear the name and Arms of Colquhoun, and the estates of Grant and Luss never be conjoined. Sir Humphry died in 1715. James Grant succeeded as Sir James Colquhoun ; but his elder brother dying without issue in 1719, he succeeded to the estate of Grant, and resuming that name, was succeeded in Luss by his second son, Sir Ludovick. He, on the death of his elder brother, unmarried, also succeeded to the estate of Grant, and that of Luss went to his younger brother, James. He was recognised as chief by Lyon Court in 1781 and created a Baronet in 1786, and, dying the same year, was succeeded by his son. Sir James, Baronet of Colquhoun and Luss, who died in 1907, was succeeded by his cousin, Sir Alan John Colquhoun,whose son, Sir Ivan Colquhoun of Luss, 7th Bt., K.T., died in 1948. His son, Sir Ivar, 8th Bt., is now Chief of the Clan. His seat is Rossdhu House, Luss.

There is a Clan Colquhoun Society, with its headquarters in Luss.

10 COLQUHOUN

CUMIN OR CUMMING

Badge :—Lus Mhic Cuimin (Cumin plant), wheat.

SEVERAL clans of Norman origin like the Frasers and Cummings arrived in Scotland about the 12–13th century. The Cummings belong to the Norman house "De Comines," a territorial name ; and Robert de Comyn was a companion of William the Conqueror. For 250 years from 1080 to 1330, the Cummins flourished in strength in Badenoch.

Sir John, the Red Cumin, was the first designed Lord of Badenoch. His son, John, the Black Lord of Badenoch, was one of the unsuccessful competitors for the Crown of Scotland in 1292.

Five years later he died a prisoner in England, leaving by his wife, sister of King John Baliol, a son, John, Lord of Badenoch, called in turn the Red Cumin, and one of the guardians of Scotland. He defeated the English at Roslin, 1302, but submitted to Edward in 1304, and became suspect of seeking the Crown as from Edward after Baliol's abdication. It is said he was on the point of betraying Robert Bruce to the King of England, when he perished under the daggers of Bruce and Kirkpatrick in the church of Dumfries on 10 February 1306. His slaughter inspired the whole clan with a desire to avenge his death. They opposed the King, who defeated them in 1308. The Earl was outlawed, and his forfeited estates were bestowed on the Keiths, Hays, and Douglases, whose good swords had helped to win the battle of Bannockburn. His only son married a daughter of the Earl of Pembroke, and died without heirs ; Jordan Cumin, a kinsman of his, who got Inverallochy from Earl Alexander, became ancestor of the Cumins of Culter, who got a charter of that barony from James III. in 1477. From Robert, younger brother of the Black Comyn, the House of of Altyre descends through Sir Richard, Hereditary Forester of Darnaway under David II., and on this house the undifferenced arms and chiefship devolved.

The old race is now represented by the Gordon-Cummings, Baronets of Gordonstoun. They inherited the name and Arms of Gordon by marriage.

The 6th Baronet and (but for the double name) present Chief of the Cummings is Sir William Gordon-Cumming of Altyre and Gordonstoun, in Moray.

11 CUMMING, HUNTING

THE CLAN DAVIDSON

Badge :—Lus nan cnàimhseag, or Braoileag
(Red Whortleberry).

THIS clan associated themselves and took protection of and under William Mackintosh (VII.) of Mackintosh prior to 1350, and have ever since been regarded as a sept of Clan Chattan.

Kinrara, in his history (1676), says : " The Davidsons styled of Invernahavon, in Badenoch, were, according to common tradition, originally a branch of the Comyns." After the downfall of the Comyns, Donald Du of Invernahavon associated himself with Clan Chattan, married a daughter of Angus (VI.) of Mackintosh, and became a leading member of Clan Chattan. The favour shown to him by the Captain of Clan Chattan roused the jealousy of another tribe, a jealousy which brought about the virtual extinction of the Davidsons.

The Davidsons, called *Clann Dà'idh* from their first known leader, David Du of Invernahavon, were chief actors in the two notable battles—Invernahavon (1370) and the North Inch of Perth (1396), and the losers in both battles.

The leading families are the Davidsons of Cantray, in Inverness, and the Davidsons of Tulloch, in Ross-shire.

About the year 1700 Alexander Davidson of Davidson, in Cromarty, married Miss Bayne, and it is stated purchased Tulloch from his father-in-law. The Baynes of Tulloch were for many generations of great position and influence in Rossshire. Tulloch Castle is of ancient date, the keep having been built in 1166, and other parts of it in 1665. A branch of this family entered the service of France in the seventeenth century having proved their descent to be noble for six generations prior to July 1629, as shown by the *Livre d'Or* in the imperial archives of France. At the clan-battle of Harlaw, 1411, the citizens of Aberdeen were led by Lord Provost Davidson, who fell in the battle.

The Davidsons are said to have been almost annihilated at the battle of the North Inch, Perth, in 1396. Davidson of Tulloch was latterly regarded as Chief.

12 DAVIDSON

THE DOUGLAS FAMILY

War Cry :—" A Douglas ! A Douglas ! "

THIS surname is territorial, from the wild pastoral dale possessed by William de Douglas, living 1174 to 1199. His eldest son, Sir Archibald, left two sons—Sir William, and Andrew, ancestor of the Morton family. Sir William died about 1274. His son was Sir William *le Hardi*, whose son, " the Good Sir James," the greatest of Bruce's captains in the War of Independence, was killed fighting against the Moors in Spain, 1330. Hugh, brother of Lord James, settled the family estates on his nephew, Sir William, in 1343.

In 1357 this Sir William was made Earl Douglas, and by marriage became Earl of Mar. He died 1384. His son, James, 2nd Earl of Douglas and Mar, fell at Otterburn, 1388. His own natural son became progenitor of the Marquesses of Queensberry, whilst he was succeeded under entail by Archibald " the Grim," 3rd Earl, natural son of " Good Sir James." The 4th Earl was created Duke of Touraine in France, and married Princess Margaret, daughter of Robert III. William, 6th Earl and 2nd Duke, was finally slain by Chancellor Crichton at the " Black Dinner " at Edinburgh Castle, 1440. William, 8th Earl, who married the " Fair Maid of Galloway," maintained magnificent sway at Threave Castle, and was killed at Stirling Castle by James II. in 1452. The earldom was forfeited when James, 9th Earl, was defeated at Arkinholm, 1455. The chiefship of this great family then fell to the Earls of Angus, of whom the 5th is celebrated as " Bell the Cat," leader of the rude barons who opposed the cultured court of James III. William, 11th Earl of Angus, was created Marquis of Douglas, 1633. A Dukedom of Douglas followed, 1703, but expired, 1761, when the " Douglas Cause " arose over succession to the vast estates. The Duke of Hamilton (paternally a Douglas) then became Earl of Angus and heir-male of the House of Douglas. He is Chief of the Hamiltons. The estates, after the great litigation known as " The Douglas Cause," devolved on the heir-female who was as Representator of the House of Douglas awarded the arms of Douglas of Douglas, and was later created Lord Douglas of Douglas, and awarded the chief Arms of the House of Douglas, whose daughter and eventual senior co-heiress married the 11th Earl of Home.

13 DOUGLAS

THE DRUMMONDS

Badge :—Cuileann (Holly).

THIS clan's name is evidently a territorial one, from the lands of Drummond or Drymen, in Stirlingshire.

Malcolm Beg, so called from his low stature, sixth of the family, Seneschal of the Lennox, married Ada, daughter of Maldowen, Earl of Lennox. His great-grandson, Sir Malcolm Drummond, was loyal to Bruce, and after Bannockburn received from him certain lands in Perthshire. Margaret de Logie, his daughter, was Queen to David II., while his son and successor, Sir John, married Mary Montifex, who brought him Cargill and Stobhall. He had a bitter feud with the Menteiths of Ruskie, in which his kinsman, Bryce Drummond, was slain, 1330. Having slain three of the Menteiths, he was compelled to resign Rosneath in compensation. After this he retired to Stobhall. His daughter, Annabella, became Queen of Robert III. His descendant, another Sir John, was in 1487 created Lord Drummond. His daughter, Margaret, James IV.'s early love, was poisoned along with her sister in 1502.

James, 4th Lord Drummond, was created Earl of Perth in 1605. James, 4th Earl was Lord Chancellor of Scotland, and followed the fortunes of James VII., who created him Duke of Perth. He died in 1716. James, his son, 2nd Duke, was married to Lady Jane Gordon. He died in 1720, and was succeeded by his elder son, John, 3rd Duke, the celebrated Jacobite leader, who was wounded at Culloden.

James, second son of David, 2nd Lord Drummond, was created Lord Maderty in 1610, and in 1686 the 4th Lord was created Viscount of Strathallan. In 1902 William, 11th Viscount, succeeded as 15th Earl of Perth. He was succeeded by his brother Eric, to whom his son succeeded in 1951 as 17th Earl and Chief of the clan with seat at Stobhall, Perthshire.

Among the principal cadets are Drummond of Hawthornden, in Midlothian ; Drummond of Concraig ; Drummond of Stanmore, in Middlesex ; and Drummond of Blair Drummond.

The tartan shown is the historic and ancient sett of the clan approved by the Chief. A version of the Grant tartan has recently sometimes been sold instead.

14 DRUMMOND

THE CLAN ERSKINE

THE name is derived from the Barony of Erskine, in Renfrew-shire, held by Henry de Erskine, in the reign of Alexander II. Sir Robert Erskine, Chamberlain of Scotland 1350–57, married Beatrix, daughter of Sir Alexander Lindsay of Crawford, by whom he had two sons—Thomas, his heir, and Malcolm, ancestor of the Erskines of Kinnoull. Sir Robert's eldest son, Thomas, married and had issue—Robert, created Lord Erskine, and John, ancestor of the Erskines of Dun.

Robert, 4th Lord Erskine, was killed at the battle of Flodden, and was succeeded by his son. James, 5th Lord, was father of John, 6th Lord Erskine who was restored as 18th Earl of Mar by Queen Mary, and was found to have received, also in 1565, a new Earldom of Mar—perhaps in case of the Crown· ever cancelling the restoration. He died in 1572, and was succeeded by his son, John, as 19th and 2nd Earl. This nobleman was twice married, and his great-great-grandson (by his first marriage), John, 23rd and 6th Earl, is well known in connection with the Scottish Rising of 1715. His descendant, John Francis Miller, 28th and 9th Earl, successfully claimed the Earldom of Kellie on the extinction of the junior branch of the family; but, dying without issue 1866, his cousin, Walter Coningsby, succeeded as 12th Earl of Kellie, and also claimed the Earldom of Mar. This claim was resisted by John Francis Erskine Goodeve, the nephew of the last (28th and 9th) Earl. In 1875 the House of Lords reported that Walter Henry, 13th Earl of Kellie (son of the 12th Earl), had made out his claim to an Earldom of Mar, dated 1565. This decision implemented an old prophecy that " The Honours of Mar would be doubled." His great-grand-son, John Francis, Earl of Mar and Kellie, is present Chief of the Erskines. His seats are Alloa and Kellie Castle. The ancient Earldom, originally mormaership, of Mar, was confirmed to John Francis, as 29th Earl, and next devolved on his sister's grandson, Lionel Walter, 31st Earl from Ruadri, Mormaer of Mar in 1115, whose cousin James Clifton of Mar is now 32nd Earl and represents the old " Tribe of Mar."

From the Erskines have also descended the Earls of Buchan and the Earls of Rosslyn. Three of the Erskine Baronets of Cambo (cr. 1663) held the office of Lord Lyon King of Arms, and Charles, 1st Bt., established the new Lyon Register in 1672.

15 ERSKINE

THE CLAN FARQUHARSON

War Cry :—" Càrn na cuimhne "
(" Cairn of Remembrance ").
Badge :—Scots Fir.

THE progenitor of the Farquharsons was Farquhar, fourth son of Alexander Ciar Shaw, 3rd of Rothiemurchus. In Aberdeenshire, the descendants of this Farquhar were called Farquharsons. Farquhar's descendant, Finlay Mòr, standard-bearer at Pinkie, where he fell, 1547, stands prominent, and from and after him the Farquharsons were termed *Clann Fhionnlaigh*, or descendants of Finlay.

In the Rising of 1715 John Farquharson of Invercauld, with four officers and 140 men, joined the Clan Chattan Regiment, in which he was Lieutenant-Colonel, and accompanying it to England, was taken prisoner at Preston, where he remained for ten months. At Culloden the Farquharsons mustered 300 men, and were in the centre of the front line.

John Farquharson, 9th of Invercauld, died in 1750, and was succeeded by his son, James, who appears to have been, in 1745, a Captain of Foot in the Hanoverian army. He died in 1806, after having been in possession of the estates for fifty-six years. He left no male issue, and was succeeded under the destination of the of the entail by his only surviving child, Catherine, who married Captain James Ross, R.N. (second son of Sir John Lockhart-Ross of, Balnagowan, Bart.), who took the name of Farquharson of Invercauld, and died in 1810. She was succeeded by her son, James, who died in 1862, and was succeeded by his son, James, 13th of Invercauld, who died 1888. His son, Alexander Haldane-Farquharson of Invercauld died 1936, and his elder daughter, Mrs Myrtle Farquharson of Invercauld, who, in virtue of the Lyon Court decree of 3rd December 1936 confirming to her the arms and the supporters of the chiefship of the Farquharsons became Chief of the clan, being killed in an air-raid 1941, was succeeded by her nephew Captain Alwyne Farquharson of Invercauld, the present chief.

Among leading cadets are Farquharson of Monaltrie, Whitehouse, Haughton, Allargue, Breda, and Finzean—all in Aberdeenshire. Joseph Farquharson of Finzean, R.A., the celebrated artist, was chieftain of that branch until 1935. Farquharson of Inverey was a celebrated cadet, one of whose chieftains, " The Black Colonel "—a Jacobite hero—lives in Deeside ballad lore.

16 FARQUHARSON

THE CLAN FERGUSSON

War Cry :—" Clannfhearghuis gu brath."
Badge :—(Dunfallandy) Crithean (Poplar).

THE house of Fergusson of Kilkerran in Ayrshire descends from Fergus MacFergus, who held his lands by charter from Robert I. Sir Adam Fergusson, 3rd Bart., died 1813, and was succeeded by his nephew, Sir James, who died in 1838. His son, Sir Charles, died in 1849, and was succeeded by his son, the Rt. Hon. Sir James Fergusson of Kilkerran, 6th Baronet, G.C.S.I., K.C.M.G., etc., who perished in the Jamaica earthquake, 1907. His son, Sir Charles, succeeded him as 7th Baronet of this line. Sir Charles, 9th Baronet, and Baron of Kilkerran holds the undifferenced arms as chief of the name.

The clan was early established in Atholl where the Chief of the Clan 'ic Fhearguis of Atholl was Fergusson of Dunfallandy, Baron of Douny and Derculich, descending from an Adam *na Cannabaig*. On the death of Archibald, grandson of General Archibald Fergusson of Dunfallandy, in 1874, the succession passed to his sister, Miss Margaret Fergusson of Dunfallandy. At her death in 1900 the succession passed to the General's great-grand-nephew, Donald S. Fergusson of Dunfallandy, whose grandson is the present Fergusson of Dunfallandy. The clan were among the gallant Atholl men who followed the banner of Montrose in the Civil War, and in 1745 the Atholl and Strathardle Fergussons were " out " with Prince Charlie.

In Argyll the Clann Fhearghuis of Stra-chur long held Glen shellich on Loch Fyne and office of Heritable Maer. The representative whose Arms are duly recorded in Lyon Court was Seumas, Chief of Clannfhearghuis of Stra-chur who died in New York.

In Aberdeenshire, where they have been landowners since the fourteenth century, among the best-known families are those of Baddifurrow, Kinmundy, and Pitfour, many of whom distinguished themselves on the Bench, at the Bar, and in Parliament. The clan also gained a footing in Banffshire and Kincardineshire as well as in Fife and Angus.

In Dumfries and Galloway the name Fergusson is one of great antiquity and the Fergussons of Craigdarroch claimed descent from Fergus, Prince of Galloway. Annie Laurie of Maxwelton married Alexander Fergusson of Craigdarroch.

17 FERGUSSON

THE CLAN FORBES

War Cry :—" Lònach " (A mountain in Strath Don).
Badge :—Bealaidh (Broom).

THE clan took its name from the Aberdeenshire parish of Forbes, where the present peer still holds part of the *duthus* or Lordship of Forbes. The clan's traditional connection with the lands of Forbes originated from a famous hunter, Oconochar, who is said to have slain a monstrous bear, and consequently this founder of the Clan took possession, as first occupier, of the district, of which his successors were allodial chiefs until the thirteenth century. The first feudal charter—converting the *duthus* of Forbes (hitherto held " under God ") into a barony—is dated 1271.

Alexander de Forbes lost his life defending the castle of Urquhart against Edward I. in 1303, but he left a son, also Alexander, who fell at the battle of Dupplin in 1332. The posthumous son of the latter, Sir John Forbes of that Ilk, had four sons, and from the three younger sprang the Forbeses of Pitsligo, Culloden, Waterton, and Foveran. He died in 1406.

Alexander, his eldest son, was raised to the Peerage by James I. as Lord Forbes. James, 2nd Lord Forbes, had three sons—William, the 3rd Lord ; Duncan, ancestor of the Forbeses of Corsindae and Monymusk ; and Patrick, ancestor of the Forbeses, Baronets of Craigievar, whose seat is the romantic tower-castle of Craigievar.

The Edinglassie Forbeses are a branch of the parent stock, and the Forbeses of Tolquhoun, a very old branch, acquired that estate in 1420, and were progenitors of the Lairds of Culloden.

Sir William Forbes, eighth Baronet of Craigievar, in 1884 succeeded his kinswoman as Lord Sempill, and was in turn succeeded in 1905 by his eldest son, Sir John Forbes Sempill.

According to the information supplied by the late Dr. W. Forbes Skene to Mr Elphinstone Dalrymple, the present Forbes tartan was designed for the Pitsligo family in 1822 by adding a white line to the Forty-Second. The old Forbes sett, of which examples survive at Newe had a simpler base.

Nigel Ivan, Lord Forbes, is now chief of the clan; his seat is Castle Forbes in Aberdeenshire.

18 FORBES

FORTY-SECOND ROYAL HIGHLAND REGIMENT

(THE BLACK WATCH)

THE origin of this gallant regiment dates as far back as 1729. The Highlands were then in an unsettled condition, and the Government entertained the idea of making use of the Highlanders as a means of protecting the country and for this purpose six companies were formed. The men were all of respectable families, and were commanded by such well-known Highlanders as Lord Lovat, Campbell of Lochnell, Grant of Ballindalloch, Campbell of Finab, Campbell of Carrick, and Munro of Culcairn. Their duties consisted in carrying out the " Disarming Act " of 1716, and preventing depredations. In 1739 the Government determined to add to their number, which was raised from 525 to 1000. It has been ascertained that from the first raising of the companies they were dressed in a special tartan, which later came to be called " the Government tartan," and has indications of being a dark sett of the " Royal " tartan. This ultimately became the well-known 42nd or Black Watch. It appears therefore that the sett was actually one authorised for Government use. John, 21st Earl of Crawford, was the first Colonel.

From the colour of the uniform of the Regular troops they were locally called *Saighdearan Dearg*—red soldiers, and the Highlanders from their sombre dress, *Freiceadan Dubh* or Black Watch.

The Black Watch since its formation has taken a brilliant part in nearly every war its country has been engaged in, and has fought with honour in every quarter of the globe.

In 1887 a memorial cairn was erected to the Black Watch on the banks of the Tay near Aberfeldy. It bears inscriptions in Gaelic and English, stating that it was erected " in commemoration of the assembling together at Tay Bridge in 1739 of the six independent companies (afterwards increased to ten) of the *Freiceadan Dubh*, or Black Watch, who, after serving in several parts of the Highlands, were embodied into a regiment designated the 43rd, and afterwards the 42nd Royal Highlanders, whose first muster took place in May 1740 near Tay Bridge."

19 FORTY-SECOND REGIMENT (BLACK WATCH)

THE CLAN FRASER

War Cry :—" A'Mhór-fhaiche " (" The Great Field ").
Badge :—Iubhar (Yew).

THE Frasers are a clan of Norman origin. The name is spelt variously as Frazer, Freser, Frezel, etc., and is referred to the old French *freze*—strawberry. Gilbert of Fraser witnessed a charter to the Monastery of Coldstream, 1109. Sir Simon Fraser of Oliver Castle was put to death by Edward I., but his brother, Alexander, carried on the line of the family. Sir Alexander Fraser, Chamberlain of Scotland, married The Bruce's sister and from him descend the Frasers of Philorth, Lord Saltoun. Sir Alexander, 9th of Philorth, on the death of his cousin, Lord Saltoun, in 1669, was served heir-of-line and his descendant, Alexander, is now 19th Lord Saltoun. Fraser of Muchal, cadet of Philorth acquired Philorth about 1619, in terms under which he was created Lord Fraser and given the undifferenced arms, but after this Lord's death it appears Lord Saltoun became heir-male and " The Fraser," whose seat is Caernbulg Castle—the old fortress of Philorth, now Fraserburgh. Sir Simon (youngest brother of Sir Alexander, the Chamberlain) was apparently the ancestor of Fraser of Lovat which bears the patronymic *MacShimie*. His grandson, Hugh of Lovat, was portioner of the Aird in 1367. His second son married the heiress of Fenton of Beaufort, and prior to 1460 her descendant had been created Lord Fraser of Lovat. Simon, 11th Lord Lovat, deeply involved in the Jacobite rising of 1745 was attainted, and executed after Culloden. Though an unprincipled man, he was a good chief, who declared " There is nothing I place in balance with my kindred "—the Fraser clansmen. His peerage was revived in 1837, when Thomas Fraser of Strichen and Lovat was created Lord Lovat, and in 1857, the attainder being reversed, he became 12th Lord Fraser of Lovat, his descendant. Simon, 15th Lord Lovat, is Chief of Clan Fraser of Lovat.

The Frasers, Baronets of Ledclune, descend from Hugh, first Lord Lovat, through Alexander, his second son.

20 FRASER, DRESS

THE CLAN GORDON

War Cry :—" A Gordon ! A Gordon ! "
Badge :—Iadh-shlat, Eitheann (Ivy).

THIS surname is territorial. Richard, Baron of Gordon in Berwickshire, about 1150-60, granted land to the monks of St. Mary at Kelso. For services at Slioch battle King Robert the Bruce gave Sir Adam Gordon the Lordship of Strathbogie in Aberdeenshire. His great-grandson, Sir Adam, was slain in battle, 1402, leaving an heiress, Elizabeth, who married Alexander, second son of Seton of Seton. Her only son, Alexander, was created Earl of Huntly in 1449. He settled the Earldom on his second son, George who took the name of Gordon and became the Chief of this *clan*, an honour which the Lyon declared in 1727 to be in the Huntly-Gordon line.

George, 4th Earl, the most powerful noble in Scotland, fell at Corrichie, 1562. In 1599 the 6th Earl was created Marquis of Huntly. George, 4th Marquis was created Duke of Gordon in 1684 by Charles II. The 2nd Duke was " out " in 1715 ; his fourth son, Lord Lewis Gordon, was a celebrated Jacobite in 1745. George, 4th Duke, and his celebrated Duchess, Jean Maxwell, raised the Gordon Highlanders. On the death of George, 5th and last Duke, in 1836, the Marquisate of Huntly went to the Earl of Aboyne, descended from George, fourth son of George, 2nd Marquis of Huntly, and is now held by Douglas, 12th Marquis, and Chief of the Gordons, whose seat is Aboyne Castle, Aberdeenshire. John Gordon of Pitlurg is male representative of the Gordons of Strathbogie, being descended from a half-brother (by a " handfast " marriage) of the heiress, and ranks as " eldest cadet."

The Earls of Aberdeen, created 1682, are descended from Patrick Gordon of Methlic (cousin of Pitlurg), who fell at the battle of Arbroath in 1445. John, 7th Earl, and 1st Marquess of Aberdeen, K.T., was Lord Lieutenant of Ireland and Governor-General of Canada. Two regiments of " Gordon Highlanders " have been raised from this clan, the old 81st, formed 1777, disbanded 1783, and the 92nd Gordon Highlanders, raised in 1794.

On the raising of the Gordon Highlanders a yellow strip was introduced into the Black Watch pattern for their regimental use, and since then the Gordons have used the red and Huntly tartans for full-dress occasions.

21 GORDON

GOW AND MACGOWAN

THE name Gow is derived from *Gobha*, a smith or armourer: the Macpherson historians aver that *Neill Cromb*, third son of Muriach, Prior of Kingussie, Chief of Clan Chattan, " was progenitor of all the name of Smith in Scotland." The Smiths (in Gaelic Gows and MacGowans) have at any rate been regarded as belonging to the Clan Chattan, and whilst some, for a romantic reason after mentioned, are especially connected with Clan Macpherson, the existence of a distinct Gow (or MacGowan) tartan appropriate to the name of *Smith* is consistent with the tradition of some of these descending from Niel, a cadet of the Clan Chattan stem, and not from the Clan Macpherson. The later connection is associated with the famous clan fight on the North Inch of Perth, 1396, where (following Froissart's chivalric analogy) a combat of " Thirty against Thirty " in the Scottish Court of Chivalry decided a point of precedence within the Clan Chattan, which Shaw, the historian of Moray, says was between Clan Dhai (claiming to be " eldest cadet " of the Clan Chattan) and Clan Macpherson (the heir-male of Gillechattan) as to which should lead Clan Chattan's right wing, a matter which had been in dispute since that position had been allowed to the Davidson Chief at the Battle of Invernahavon in 1370. One of the Macphersons took ill, and a Perth smith, " Hal o' the Wynd," undertook to join the Macphersons who eventually won with ten survivors and the smith (whose descendants were of course received into Clan Macpherson), whilst the only surviving Davidson saved himself by swimming the Tay. That the contestants were the Davidsons and Macphersons, and that the latter won, seems borne out by the admission that Macpherson was ever after allowed the principal place on the right of the Chief of the Clan Chattan. Only Trial by Combat could have resulted in this honour passing to the " heir-male " and not remaining with the " eldest cadet." The incident, as arising out of a chivalric decree, is an important point in Scottish Clan law and as regards the history of Clan Chattan.

The Gow tartan is that appropriate to the name of Smith and its variants.

22 GOW AND MACGOWAN

THE CLAN GRAHAM

Badge :—Buaidh-chraobh, na Labhras (Laurel).

THE patriotic race of Graham claims traditional descent from Grame, a Caledonian chief who expelled the Romans ; but the first authentic ancestor seems to be William of Graham, one of the witnesses of David I.'s Holyrood Charter, 1143–47. He afterwards obtained the lands of Abercorn and Dalkeith. His great-grandson, Sir David Graham, acquired Dundaff from Patrick, Earl of Dunbar ; and Strathblane and Mugdock from the Earl of Lennox. He had three sons—Sir Patrick, Sir David, and Sir John, termed " the right hand " of the patriot Wallace, who fell at the battle of Falkirk, 1298. Sir Patrick his heir, " a goodly knight," fell in defence of Scotland at Dunbar, 1296. His son, Sir David, signed the letter to the Pope, 1320, and got from The Bruce a charter of Old Montrose, 1325. His descendant, Sir William, *Dominus de Graham et Kincardine*, obtained from Robert, Duke of Albany, a charter of entail of Old Montrose. Patrick, his grandson, was created Lord Graham by James II about 1445. William, 3rd Lord, was created Earl of Montrose by James IV. in 1503. He fell at Flodden. James, 5th Earl and 1st Marquis, was the illustrious Royalist, and Lieutenant of Scotland for Charles I., who after several glorious campaigns on behalf of the Scottish Crown was executed by the Parliament, 1650. John Graham of Claverhouse, Viscount of Dundee, greatest of Jacobite commanders, fell at Killiecrankie in command of the army of James VII.

The Grahams of the Borders are descended from Sir John Graham of Kilbride, second son of Malise, Earl of Strathearn, and afterwards of Menteith. Sir John was ancestor of the Grahams of Gartmore, in Perthshire.

James, 4th Marquis, was cr. Duke of Montrose 1707 ; and to James, 3rd Duke, K.T. (when M.P. and Marquis of Graham), Highlanders are indebted for an Act in 1782 repealing the disgraceful Statute of 1747, which made penal the use of the Highland garb. The Chief of the clan is James Angus, 7th Duke of Montrose.

Graham of Menteith, an historic branch, held the Earldoms of Airth, Menteith and Strathearn. Their tartan is given in Johnston's *Scottish Tartans*.

23 GRAHAM OF MONTROSE

THE CLAN GRANT

War Cry :—" Stand fast, Craigellachie."
Badge :—Giuthas (Pine Tree).

THIS clan is one of the principal branches of the " siol Alpine " and the muir of *Griantach* in Strathspey may be the origin of the clan's name. The first Grants mentioned in Scottish records are Lawrence and Robert le Grant in 1258. Sir Lawrence was Sheriff of Inverness, and Robert held lands in Nairnshire. Stratherrick and Inverallen belonged to the clan in the fourteenth century, but *Ian Ruadh*, Sheriff of Inverness, 1434, is the first Chief from whom an unbroken descent is deducible. The lands of Freuchie were erected into a Regality of Grant, and the chiefs were long known as " The Lairds of Grant," refusing even an Earldom of Strathspey so as not to supersede their chiefly title.

John Grant of Freuchie and Grant married, in 1484, a daughter of Ogilvie of Deskford, and left James, his successor, ancestor of the Earls of Seafield ; and John, on whom he bestowed the Barony of Corrimony in 1509, from whom descends Sir Francis, K.C.V.O., Lord Lyon King of Arms. James Grant of that Ilk, 3rd Baron of Freuchie, *Sheumas nan Creach*, and his son, John, the next chief, were supporters of Mary, Queen of Scots.

Sir James Grant of that Ilk and his son, Ludovic, 8th Laird of Freuchie, adhered to William II. of Scotland (or Orange), and were with the clan in the fight at the Haughs of Cromdale. In 1715 and 1745 he adhered to the House of Hanover, but Glenmoriston was " out " for the Stewarts. The marriage of Ludovic to Margaret, daughter of James, Earl of Seafield, brought that title into the family in the person of her grandson, Sir Lewis Alexander Grant of Grant.

There are three Baronets of the surname—Dalvey 1688, Monymusk, 1705, and Ballindalloch, 1838.

The 11th Earl of Seafield died of wounds received in action, 12th November 1915, and was succeeded in his Scottish Peerages by his daughter, Nina Caroline, Countess of Seafield, while the late Earl's brother, Sir Trevor Ogilvie Grant, succeeded to the Barony of Strathspey and chiefship of Clan Grant. His son Patrick, 5th Lord Strathspey, is 32nd Chief of the Clan.

24 GRANT

THE CLAN GUNN

Badge :—Aitionn (Juniper) or Lus nan laoch (Roseroot).

THIS clan is of Norse origin. The Gunns were a warlike clan of Caithness and Sutherland ; the name is derived from the Norse word *gunnr*—war.

The Gunns and the Keiths were for ever at enmity. Lachlan Gunn of Braemore had an only daughter, Helen, who was famous for her beauty, and the day of her marriage with her cousin Alexander was fixed ; but Dugald Keith, a retainer of Keith of Ackergill, whose advances she had repelled, surrounded her father's house with a body of armed Keiths, slew many of the Gunns, who were unprepared for an attack, and carried off the girl to Ackergill, where she became the victim of her abductor, and eventually threw herself from the summit of the tower.

Raid upon raid ensued now, and during one of these, in 1426, a desperate battle was fought between the two clans at Harpsdale, eight miles from Thurso. The conflict was rancorous and bloody, but indecisive.

About the middle of the fifteenth century, the Chief of the clan was George, who lived with barbaric pomp in his castle at Clyth. From the office he held he was known as Crouner Gunn, but by the natives as " *Am Bràisteach Mór*," from a large silver brooch which fastened his plaid (being the badge of his office of Coroner of Caithness). Weary of the feud, he and the Chief of the Keiths agreed to meet with twelve horsemen a-side at the Chapel of St. Tears and settle it amicably. This was in 1464. The Keiths came with twenty-four men—two on each horse— and attacked the Gunns ; the latter fought desperately and were cut to pieces. George Gunn was slain and stripped of his arms, armour, and brooch. Soon after William MacKames, a kinsman of the Gunns, killed George of Ackergill and his son, with ten men, at Drummay.

The patronymic of Gunn of Kilearnan is *Mac-Sheumais Chataich*.

The chiefship is dormant, but a Clan Society has been founded to seek the heir.

25 GUNN

THE CLAN HAMILTON

Badge :—Bay Leaves.

THE founder of this family was Walter, son of Gilbert de Hameldone, to whom Bruce gave the Barony of Cadzow in Lanarkshire, celebrated as the home of the old white Caledonian cattle. Sir James the Hamilton, Lord of Cadzow under James II, was in 1445 created Lord Hamilton. By his second wife, Princess Mary, sister of James III, he had James, 2nd Lord, created Earl of Arran, 1502, whose son James, 2nd Earl, the Regent Arran of Mary Queen of Scots' childhood, founded Hamilton Palace, and was declared by Parliament, after her, next heir to the throne. He was created Duke of Chatelherault in France and married Lady Margaret Douglas, daughter of the 3rd Earl of Morton. Their son John became Marquis of Hamilton, 1599, and James, 3rd Marquis, his grandson, became Duke of Hamilton, 1643, and Hereditary Keeper of the Palace of Holyroodhouse, a title which has remained in the family ever since. An active Royalist, he was beheaded in 1649, and was succeeded by his brother William, 2nd Duke, who died in defence of Charles II at Worcester, 1651. The Dukedom reverted to his niece, Anne, 3rd Duchess of Hamilton, who married Lord William Douglas, Earl of Selkirk; they were created Duke and Duchess of Hamilton in 1663, the Earldom of Selkirk being transferred to their second son. The eldest son James, 4th Duke, patriotically opposed the Union, 1707, and was shortly after killed by an English peer, Lord Mohun. William, 12th Duke, was in 1864 confirmed by Napoleon III in the French duchy of Chatelherault. Alfred, 13th Duke, after the demolition of Hamilton Palace, removed the seat of the chiefs to Dungavel in their Lordship of Avon. The Duke of Hamilton is Chief of the family.

26 HAMILTON

THE CLAN HAY

WILLIAM DE HAYA, progenitor of this Clan, was cupbearer to Malcolm IV. and married Eva, Lady of Petmulin. About 1178, he received the Barony of Erroll. Tradition associates the Hays with a victory over the Danes at a battle of Luncarty, on which history is silent. Sir Gilbert, 5th of Erroll, a faithful adherent of The Bruce, was created Hereditary Constable of Scotland. Sir Thomas, 4th High Constable, married Princess Elizabeth, daughter of Robert II., and from their second son, Sir Gilbert of Dronlaw, descend the Hays of Delgaty, of whom Sir Arthur, 10th Bt. of Park, seems heir-male of the race. Sir William, 5th Lord High Constable, was grandfather of William, created Earl of Erroll 1452 ; his descendant William, 6th Earl, had an only daughter, Jean, wife of the 8th Earl, the honours meantime passed to her cousin and father-in-law, George Hay of Logie. Francis, 9th Earl joined Lord Huntly and defeated Argyll at Glenlivet, 1594. Gilbert, 11th Earl. having no issue, executed an entail on his cousin, Sir John Hay of Kellour, 12th Earl. Charles, 13th Earl, imprisoned as a Jacobite, dying unmarried, was succeeded (even in his military office of High Constable of Scotland) by his sister Mary, Countess of Erroll (described as Chief of the family of Hay) an ardent Jacobite. Her sister, Margaret, Countess of Linlithgow, had a daughter married to the Jacobite Earl of Kilmarnock, who was executed 1746, but her son James succeeded his great-aunt as 15th Earl of Erroll and Constable, and took the name of Hay. William George, 18th Earl's magnificence as Lord High Constable to George IV. in 1822, eventually caused the sale of Slains Castle. Josslyn Victor, 22nd Earl, was in 1941 succeeded by his daughter Diana, Countess of Erroll, who is now Hereditary High Constable of Scotland and Chief of the Hays.

From the Hays of Locherwort and Yester, derive the Marquises of Tweeddale, whose seat is Yester in East Lothian, where the old castle includes the celebrated " Goblin Ha' " ; from another branch, Hay of Megginch and Kinfauns, descends the Earl of Kinnoull.

Slains Castle, the seat of the Chiefs of Clan Hay, stands on the Aberdeenshire coast. Delgaty Castle, Turriff, Aberdeenshire, is a Clan Hay centre.

27 HAY

THE HENDERSONS

(MacKendricks).

Badge :—Canach (Cotton Grass).

THE Hendersons claim descent from *Eanruig Mór Mac Righ Neachtan*—Big Henry, son of King Nectan. It is difficult to determine when the descendants of *Eanruig Mór* became possessed of that tract of country embracing Glencoe, both sides of Loch Leven and Ardnamurchan. According to tradition, the Chiefs of the Clan held their seats at Callart, on the north side of Loch Leven, and as late as the fifteenth century a chieftain of the clan held the lands of Callart. The Glencoe Hendersons clung to their lands under the vassalage of the Lords of the Isles, and were known generally as the *MacIains* of Glencoe, a name applied to them through their first Chief of the MacDonald line, "*Iain Fraoch*," who flourished in 1346. He was brother of John, 1st Lord of the Isles, and natural son of Angus Og of Islay. Gregory says : "Angus Og had a natural son, known as *Iain Fraoch*, or Heather John, on whom his brother, John, Lord of the Isles, bestowed Glencoe." *Iain Fraoch's* mother was, it is understood, a daughter of Dugald MacHendry—*i.e.* Dugald Henderson—a former headman of Glencoe, and according to the old Scottish law of succession, the Chiefship passed down to her son. They lived at Inverlochy for a time, where their first son and heir was born, who in due time became the first MacIain of Glencoe, or, as the Glencoe people called him, *Iain Abrach* (John of Lochaber). *Iain Fraoch* appointed Hendersons as his bodyguard, and until the death of the last MacIain Chief they were accorded the honour of the first " lift " of the remains when borne forth for burial.

The Hendersons of Caithness have no connection with those of Glencoe. They are descendants of Hendry, son of George Gunn, Crouner of that county. There are also Hendersons in Fordell, Fifeshire, who claim as a cadet of their family Alexander Henderson, the great divine and leader of the Reformation. The old castle of Fordell was recently bought by a Henderson from the Mercer-Henderson Earls of Buckinghamshire.

28 HENDERSON

THE CLAN INNES

Badge :—Bulrush.

THE Clan Innes derives from Berowald, to whom in 1160,
" after agreement between the King and Somerled " (of the
Isles), King Malcolm IV. granted the Barony of Innes in Moray.
In 1579 the Privy Council recognised the Inneses as a " clan."
Sir Alexander, 9th of that Ilk, married Janet, heiress of the thane
of Aberchirder. Sir James, 12th Chief, was Esquire to James III.
and entertained James IV. at Innes, 1490. William, 15th Chief
sat in the Reformation Parliament, 1560 ; his son Alexander,
16th Chief, was beheaded by the Regent Morton, and John,
17th, resigned his chiefship to Alexander Innes of Cromey,
grand-nephew of the 13th. Sir Robert, 20th Chief, a prominent
Covenanter, was created a Baronet 1625, and welcomed Charles
II. at Garmoch 1650. Sir James Innes of that Ilk, 6th Bt. and
25th Chief, succeeded as 5th Duke of Roxburghe 1805. His
son was created Earl Innes in 1836. George, 9th Duke, is 4th
Earl Innes, 10th Bt., and 29th Chief.

Walter of Innermarkie, 1486, was second son of Sir Robert,
11th Chief. Robert, 2nd of Innermarkie was Hereditary
Constable of Redcastle. He married Lady Elspeth Stewart of
Atholl, niece of King James II. Sir Robert, 5th laird, acquired
Balvenie, 1615, and was created Baronet, 1628. Sir Robert, 6th
Bt., enlisted in the Scots Greys and married the Colonel's
daughter. Sir William, 8th Bt., was succeeded by Sir John
Innes, 9th Bt. and 9th Laird of Edingight, whose father was
" out " with Prince Charlie. Sir Walter Innes, 15th Bt. of
Balvenie, represents this branch.

The Baronets of Coxton (cr. 1686), a branch of Innermarkie,
" out " in all the Jacobite Risings, held Coxton Tower, a remark-
able fortalice near Elgin.

Father Lewis Innes, Lord Almoner to the Chevalier and
Jacobite Secretary of State for Scotland, 1690, and his brother,
Father Thomas, the historian, descended from Robert of
Drainie, third son of the 11th Chief. From Innes of Benwall
sprang Robert of Blairton, Lyon Depute in 1672, when the
present Lyon Register was instituted. The fortune of George,
of Stow, the millionaire banker, passed to the Mitchell-Inneses.
John Innes, Bishop of Moray, 1407–14, rebuilt Elgin Cathedral
after the " Wolf of Badenoch," burnt it.

29 INNES

THE CLAN JOHNSTON

Badge :—Red Hawthorn.

THIS is one of the Border clans, whose origin goes back to the thirteenth century in the person of Sir Gilbert de Johnstoun, son of John, who lived about 1200. He had a son, Gilbert, who was father of Sir John, living 1296. Sir John was father of John and Gilbert de Johnstoun ; the latter was succeeded by his son, Sir John. The last named had one son, Adam, who was ancestor of the Johnstons of Newbie, Mylnefield, and Galabank. The above Adam Johnston was twice married, and had by his first wife a son, John, ancestor of the Johnstons of Westerhall, and by his second wife he had Sir Gilbert, ancestor of the Johnstons of Elphinstone. Sir James of Johnstone was created Lord Johnstone, 1633, and Earl of Hartfell, 1643. His son, James, was created Earl of Annandale and Hartfell, 1661. The 2nd Earl was succeeded by his son, William, who was created Marquess of Annandale, 1701. He was twice married. By his first marriage he had James, 2nd Marquess, who died without issue 1730, and Henrietta, who married Charles, first Earl of Hopetoun ; she is now represented by Hope-Johnstone of Annandale, chief of the Border Johnstons, whose seat is Raehills, Lockerbie. By his second marriage, the 1st Marquess had George, 3rd Marquess, who died 1792. From Matthew, 1st of Westerhall, descended Sir James, who died 1699. He left two sons, Sir John, who died without issue, and his brother, Sir William, who left two sons, Sir James, 3rd Baronet of Westerhall, and John, whose son, Richard, was created a Baronet in 1795, whose grandson, Harcourt, 3rd Baronet, was created Baron Derwent, 1881. The 3rd Baronet of Westerhall left six sons. John, fifth son, was the ancestor of the Johnstones of Alva. The North Country Johnstones descend from Stephen the clerk, who married Margaret, daughter and heiress of Sir Andrew Garioch of Caskieben, which last became their style. He is now represented by Sir Thomas Alexander Johnston (13th Baronet) of Caskieben, who is settled in the U.S.A.

30 JOHNSTON

THE CLAN KENNEDY

Badge :—Oak.

THE Kennedys were " Captains of the Clan Muintircasduff," *i.e.* " the black-footed men " ; and they apparently spring from a branch of the Pictish Lords of Galloway, deriving from Gilbert, father of Duncan, 1st Earl of Carrick, whose son Neil, 2nd Earl, exercising his powers of Tanistry, settled the chiefship and heritable Bailiery of Carrick (which Bailiery included the subsidiary office of " leading the men of Carrick " as distinct from the chiefship, or *kenkynol*) upon a kinsman, Roland de Carrick, who appears to have married one of the Earl's daughters and died before 1275. From his grandson, Gilbert de Carrick, this *kenkynol* (chiefship) seems to have been transmitted (evidently *jure uxoris*) to John Kennedy of Dunure prior to 1357. He acquired Cassilis, by purchase or marriage, from Marjory Montgomery, and another wife is understood to have been Mary de Carrick, with whom his descendants apparently inherited the *kenkynol*. The destination was soon after changed from " heirs " to " heirs-male " by Royal Charter. His son, Sir Gilbert Kennedy of Dunure, was father of James of Dunure, who married Princess Mary, daughter of Robert III. Their son, Gilbert, was made Lord Kennedy, 1457, and David, 3rd Lord Kennedy, was created Earl of Cassilis 1509. Gilbert, 2nd Earl, was assassinated 1527. Gilbert, 3rd Earl, was one of the ambassadors poisoned at Dieppe for protecting the Scottish Royal succession in Mary Queen of Scots' marriage contract. John, 4th Earl, " a very greedy man," was celebrated for " roasting the Abbot of Crossraguel " in order to force him to sign a gift of his Abbey in favour of the Earl. His son John, 5th Earl, having married an old woman for her wealth, had no issue and was succeeded by his nephew the 6th Earl, whose Countess, Lady Jean Hamilton, was the reputed lover of Sir John Faa, the gipsy. On the death of John, 8th Earl, the honours passed to the heir-male, Sir Thomas Kennedy of Culzean, a descendant of the 3rd Earl. Archibald, 12th Earl, was created Marquis of Ailsa 1806, so that the chief of Clan Kennedy is now the Marquis of Ailsa. The chief's seats are Culzean Castle, and Cassilis, in Ayrshire.

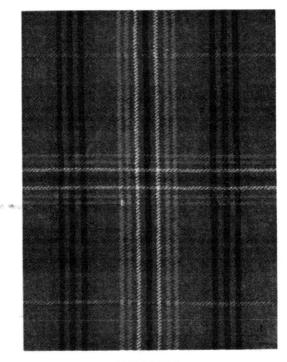

31 KENNEDY

THE CLAN KERR

Badge :—Moss Myrtle.

JOHN KERR of the Forest of Selkirk, living 1357, was father of Henry, Sheriff of Roxburgh, whose son, Robert, was father of Andrew of Auldtounburn. This Andrew Kerr had three sons. From the youngest came the Kerrs of Gateshaw, and from the second the Kerrs of Linton. The eldest son was father of Walter of Cessford, who had two sons. From the younger descended the Kerrs of Dolphinstoun, Littledean, and Morriston. The elder, Sir Robert of Caverton, died in his father's lifetime, leaving two sons—George of Faudonside, and Sir Andrew, who succeeded his grandfather in Cessford. Sir Andrew had three sons. From the first are descended the Dukes of Roxburgh. The second had a son, Mark, who was created Earl of Lothian, 1606, but the title became extinct in 1624. The third son of Sir Andrew of Cessford was ancestor to Sir Thomas of Ferniehirst, whose son by his first marriage, was created Lord Jedburgh, 1622, and by his second marriage had two sons—Sir James, whose son became Lord Jedburgh, and Robert, Earl of Somerset, 1613. Robert of Ancrum, uncle of above-named Sir Thomas, had two grandsons—William, from whom descended the Kerrs of Linton, and Sir Robert, created Earl of Ancrum, 1633, and was succeeded in the title by the son of his second marriage, Charles; his grandson by his first marriage, Robert 4th Earl of Lothian, Lord Justice-General, also succeeded to the Earldom of Ancrum, and was created Marquess of Lothian, 1701. His direct descendant is Peter Francis, 12th Marquess and chief of the clan, whose seat is Monteviot at Ancrum, Roxburghshire.

32 KERR

THE CLAN LAMONT

Badge :—Craobh-ubhal fhiadhain (Crab-apple tree).

THE surname Lamont or Lamond is from the Norse *lagamadr*—a lawman. The Lamont chiefs held their lands in Argyll from the dawn of the clan until the beginning of the present century.

The first clan of whom there is absolute historical evidence is Ferchar, who flourished about 1200. Ferchar's grandson, Laumun, was the first to use the name which has since become hereditary. About 1238 Duncan, son of Ferchar, and this Laumun, son of Malcolm, son of Ferchar, granted certain lands at Kilmun, etc., to the monks of Paisley.

About 1646 the Lamont country was ravaged by the Campbells who carried about two hundred prisoners to Dunoon and massacred them at the Gallowhill. A memorial to commemorate the event was erected by the Clan Lamont Society in 1906. In 1472 the chief's *duthus* of Inveryne was erected into a feudal barony.

From the thirteenth to the seventeenth century the chiefs used the barony title of " Inveryne," with Toward Castle for part of that time as principal residence. In 1646 Ardlamont became the seat of the Chief.

The Lamonts of Knockdow claim descent from Geoffrey (or Gorre), son of John Lamont, alive in 1431, and were allowed to matriculate arms as cadets.

In the eighteenth century the chiefship passed through Margaret, daughter of Dugald Lamont of Lamont to her son Archibald whose descendant, John Harry Lamont of that Ilk, was accorded the chief arms as heir-of-line in 1909. He sold Ardlamont, and died unmarried, when the Chiefship passed to the Monydrain branch ; and on the death of Ronald Coll (24th Chief), his daughter Mercean (25th) and cousin Keith (26th) resigned the Chiefship to his next cousin, Alfred S. Lamont of Lamont, 27th Chief 1953. The present Chief, Peter N. Lamont of Lamont, resides in N.S.W., Australia.

There is a Clan Lamont Society, founded in 1895. Its headquarters are in Glasgow.

33 LAMONT

THE CLAN LESLIE

Badge :—Rue.

THIS surname is derived from the lands of Leslie, in Aberdeenshire. The first of the name on record was Bartholf of Leslie in the reign of William the Lion.

David, 8th of Leslie, was one of the hostages for the ransom of James I. in 1424. George, 10th of Leslie, was the 1st Earl of Rothes, and was so created by James II. William, 3rd Earl, fell with his Royal master at Flodden. George, 4th Earl, accompanied James V. to France. His son, Norman, Master of Rothes, after being engaged in the murder of Cardinal Beaton, was slain in battle in Picardy in 1554. The Earl died at Dieppe in 1558. John, 7th Earl of Rothes, carried the Sword of State at the Coronation of Charles II. in Scone Palace, 1651. In 1680 he was created Duke of Rothes, but he died the following year, leaving a daughter, the Countess, whose eldest son, John succeeded by entail to the Earl of Rothes, while Thomas, her second son, carried on the honours of Haddington. Malcolm, 20th Earl of Rothes, is the present chief of the Clan and still holds part of the ancient Castlehill of Rothes in Strathspey.

Sir Alexander Leslie (1st Earl of Leven in 1641) was a famous warrior. His title is now united with that of Melville.

Sir Patrick Leslie of Pitcairlie, second son of the 5th Earl of Rothes, was created Lord Lindores by James VI. in 1600. His title has been dormant since 1775.

A famous branch were the Leslies of Balquhain, in Aberdeenshire. Sir George, the founder of it, got a grant of that estate from David II. by charter, dated 1340. Of this line came Count Leslie, who assassinated Wallenstein.

Sir Andrew Leslie, 3rd of Balquhain, had a bitter feud with the Forbeses. He was slain 1420. Sir William, 7th of Balquhain, rebuilt the castle of that name, which was burned by the Forbeses. Balquhain Castle still belongs to the baronial-chieftain, but later Barons of Balquhain, who were also Counts Leslie, lived at the Palace of Fetternear on Donside. Leslie of Wardis is Balquhain's most important cadet. Leslie of Warthill, cadet of Wardis, held that estate 1518-1956. A cadet of this line became Prince-Bishop of Laibach in Austria.

34 LESLIE, HUNTING

THE LINDSAYS

Badge :—Lime Tree.

THE name Lindsay is an old English one, denoting "Lime Tree Isle," of which there were two—one in Lincoln and one in Essex. From the place-name came the surname Lindsay, originally De Lindsay. The family came early to Scotland, and were there established in David I.'s time.

Sir David Lindsay of Crawford was living about 1340. He had two sons : (1) Alexander of Glenesk, father of David, created Earl of Crawford 1398 ; and (2) Sir William of the Byres. The grandson of the 1st Earl—David, 3rd Earl—left two sons—Alexander, 4th Earl, and Walter of Edzell. On the death of the 16th Earl, the title went to the Lindsays of the Byres, passing over the Edzell family.

David, 9th Earl of Crawford, left two sons : (1) Sir David of Edzell, whose line failed in 1744 ; and (2) John of Balcarres, father of David, created Lord Lindsay of Balcarres 1633, whose son, Alexander, was created Earl of Balcarres 1651. This Earl's grandson, James, 5th Earl of Balcarres, left two sons, the elder being Alexander, 6th Earl, who became 23rd Earl of Crawford, 1808, on the failure of the direct line of Lindsay of Byres. The present chief is David Robert Alexander, K.T., 28th Earl of Crawford and Balcarres, whose seat is Balcarres in Fife.

The Lindsays, known as "The Lightsome Lindsays," are about the only Lowland clan who have formed themselves into a Society. This they did in October 1897, under the presidency of the Right Hon. The Earl of Crawford, K.T., Chief of the clan. From Sir William, fourth son of the 6th Baron of Crawford, sprang the line of Lord Lindsay of the Byres, of which John, 10th Lord, was created Earl of Lindsay 1633. Sir David Lindsay of the Mount, Lord Lyon King of Arms and poet, was a cadet of this line.

To the Clan Lindsay we are indebted for that exquisite song, "Auld Robin Gray," which is the composition of Lady Anne Lindsay, eldest daughter of James Lindsay, 5th Earl of Balcarres. She was born 1750.

The headquarters of the Clan Society are in Edinburgh, with a branch in Glasgow.

35 LINDSAY

THE CLAN MACALISTER

Badge :—Fraoch gorm (Common Heath).

IT is generally understood that this clan branched off from the main Clan Donald stem early in the thirteenth century, descending from Alister Mor, son of Donald de Ile, and younger brother of Angus Mor ; and this is indicated by the arms matriculated for MacAlister of Loup.

In 1366, Ranald, son of Alexander, appears on the scene as heir to Clan Alister. Ranald had his residence in Kintyre where the Clan Alister at a later time are found largely to abound. In 1481 Charles MacAlister was appointed by James III. to the Stewartry of Kintyre, and at the same time received a charter for a considerable grant of lands in that peninsula. Charles was succeeded by his son, John, who is styled " John of the Lowb," now rendered Loup, from the Gaelic *lùb*, a curve or bend, this being the configuration of the shore which bounded the ancient patrimony of the Clan Alister.

During the fifteenth and sixteenth centuries members of the clan obtained settlements in Bute and Arran, and their descendants are there to this day.

In the latter half of the sixteenth century a new branch of Clan Alister of Kintyre sprung into existence—namely, the family of Tarbert. The heads of the House became hereditary Constables of Tarbert Castle. To this branch belonged Sir Donald MacAlister, Principal of Glasgow University. Another Kintyre branch are the MacAlisters of Glenbarr Abbey.

Gory Macalester of Loup had a son, Alexander, who succeeded him. He fought at Killiecrankie, under Viscount Dundee, and afterwards served with the Royal army in Ireland against William of Orange. His son died without issue, so he was succeeded by his brother, Charles, who married a daughter of Lamont of that Ilk. His son, Charles, born in 1765, married the heiress of Kennox, in Ayrshire.

The late Chief of the clan was Lieut.-Col. Charles Godfrey Somerville MacAlester of the Loup, who succeeded in 1903 and died in 1960.

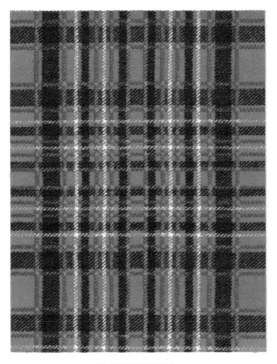

36 MACALISTER

THE MACALPINES

War Cry :—" Cuimhnich bàs Ailpein " (" Remember the death
of Alpin ").
Badge :—Giuthas (Pine Tree).

WHILE the personal name Alpin or Alpine is from the Welsh, it
came into the Gaelic from Strathclyde and from the Picts as well.
" The general appellation of *Sìol Ailpein*," says Skene in his
Highlanders of Scotland, " has been usually given to a number of
clans situated at considerable distance from each other, but who
have hitherto been supposed to possess a common descent, and
that from Kenneth MacAlpine, the ancestor of a long line of
Scottish kings. These clans are the Clan Gregor, the Grants,
the Mackinnons, Macquarries, Macnabs, and MacAulays, and
they have at all times claimed the distinction of being the noblest
and most ancient of the Highland clans. ' *Is rioghail mo dhream* '
(' My race is Royal ') was the proud motto of the MacGregors,
and although the other clans have for centuries acquiesced in
the justice of that motto, yet this lofty boast must fall before a
rigid examination into its truth ; for the authority of the
Manuscript of 1450 puts it beyond all doubt that the origin was
altogether unknown at that period, and that these clans in reality
formed part of the tribe of Ross." The principal tribe was
always admitted to be that of Clan Gregor.

That the MacAlpines are of ancient origin is maintained by
the Gaelic saying, " *Cnuic 'is uillt 'is Ailpeinich* " (" Hills and
streams and MacAlpines "), the inference being that the origin of
the MacAlpines was contemporary with the formation of hillocks
and streams.

An ancient Gaelic slogan of Early Scottish Royalists was
" *Cuimhnich bàs Ailpein* " (" Remember the death of Alpin "),
alluding to the murder of King Alpin.

37 MACALPINE

THE MACARTHURS

War Cry :—" Eisd ! O Eisd ! " (" Listen ! O Listen ! ").
   Badge :—Roid (Wild Myrtle) or Garbhag an t-sléibhe
                  (Fir Club Moss).

THE Clan Arthur is one of the oldest of the clans of Argyll ; and
its *duthus* was on the shores of Loch Awe, where its chief also
held Innestrarynich. This particular clan was known from
others of the name of Arthur as the *Clann-Artair-na-tir-a-*
chladich—" of the shore-land." So long had they been seated
there that even in Celtic days they gave rise to a celebrated
couplet :

> " *Cnuic 'is uillt 'is Ailpeinich*
>   *Ach cuin a thaing Artairich ?* "

> " The hills and streams and MacAlpine—
>   But whence came forth MacArthur ? "

The title *Mac-ic-Artair* suggests that the Clan Arthur of
Tirracladich were originally a branch of a major line (which of
course would be the case if their ancestor was a son of the " King
Arthur " of Romance, as they duly claim !) Their slogan was
" *Eisd ! O Eisd !* " (" Listen ! O Listen ! ").

Staunch supporters of the Bruce, *Mac-ic-Artair* was rewarded
with grants of land forfeited by the Macdougalls, but a century
later their influential position was lost. Ian, Chief of the Clan
Artair of Tirracladich, was one of the chiefs of Argyll put to
death by James I.; and from this disaster they never recovered.

There has been a good deal of confusion between the fore-
going Clan Arthur, and another of the same patronymic, the
MacArthur-Campbells, one of the branches of the Clan Campbell,
of whom there are many tales.

A family of MacArthurs were for many generations hereditary
pipers to the MacDonalds of Sleat. The most celebrated of the
family was Charles, whose musical education was perfected by
Patrick Og MacCrimmon.

It is maintained that the chiefship of the clan rests in the
family of the MacArthurs of Proaig, Islay, some of whose
ancestors were armourers to the MacDonalds of Islay.

38 MACARTHUR

THE CLAN MACAULAY

Badge :—Muileag (Cranberry) or Giuthas (Pine Tree).

THERE were two Clans MacAulay. The best known were the MacAulays of Ardincaple, in Dunbartonshire, a property disposed of by the 12th Chief in the eighteenth century to the Campbells of Argyll. They have no connection with the Lewis Clan MacAulay. The MacAulays of Ardincaple are believed to be of the family of Lennox, for in a charter granted by Maldowen, Earl of Lennox, to Sir Patrick Grahame, is Aulay, the Earl's brother, as also in another charter by the same Earl to William, son of Arthur Galbraith, the witnesses are Duncan and Aulay, the Earl's brothers.

Sir Aulay MacAulay of Ardincaple appears in 1587 in the Roll of the Landlords and Bailies in the Highlands and Isles as one of the principal vassals of the Earl of Lennox.

The last portion of the territory clan passed out of the hands of the 12th Chief in 1767, when Ardincaple was sold to the Duke of Argyll.

The first MacAulay of Lewis on record is Donald *Cam*, mentioned in 1610, who is said to have been captured along with Torquil Dubh in 1597, but escaped. Donald Cam's son, Angus of Brenish, was killed at Auldearn Battle, 1645. His son, Dugald, succeeded him as *Fear Bhrenis*, and his son was Rev. Aulay MacAulay, minister of Harris, married to Rev. Kenneth Morrison's daughter, of Stornoway. His son was the Rev. John Macaulay of Cardross, whose son, Zachery, was father of Lord Macaulay (cr. 1857), who in his writings besmirched the Highlanders.

The Lewis MacAulays had namesakes, no doubt kinsmen, on the mainland, vassals to the MacKenzies. Lochbroom is said to have been their original possession, a district which the heiress of Duncan MacAulay is said to have given with her hand to the Chief of the MacKenzies in the fourteenth century. The MacAulays of the mainland are coupled with the Macleays and MacIvors in the fifteenth century as giving trouble to the Earl of Ross and his tenants.

39 MACAULAY

THE MACCALLUMS OR MALCOLMS

Badge :—Rowan Berries.

THE district of Lorn, Argyllshire, is generally regarded as the habitat of the MacCallums. The personal name *Calum* is from Columba, and was, it is said, of old *Maol Caluim*—Devotee of Columba—and, later, Malcolm.

Colgin, about three miles and a half out of Oban, has long been stated to have been the headquarters of the MacCallums, and that the chief family of Colgin formed the stem of the MacCallum clan and that in later years the name was changed to Malcolm.

The most important branch of the clan and that of which there is historical record, and whose ensigns armorial are on record in the Court of the Lord Lyon, is Malcolm of Poltalloch, Chief of the Clan Challum of Ariskeodnish.

In 1562 Donald M'Gillespie vic O'Challum was seized in the lands of Poltalloch, and was the lineal ancestor of Neil Malcolm of Poltalloch, who succeeded his cousin, Dugald, in 1787 and died in 1802. His son, Neil, the next Laird, received arms and supporters in Lyon Court 1818. John Wingfield Malcolm of Poltalloch was created Lord Malcolm in 1896, and died in 1902. He was succeeded in the estate by his brother, whose son, Sir Ian Malcolm of Poltalloch, K.C.M.G., died in 1944. His heir is Lt.-Col. George Ian Malcolm of Poltalloch whose fortress is Duntroon Castle in Argyll.

Another branch of the clan, settled in Fife, descends from John Malcolm of Balbedie, Chamberlain of Fife to Charles I. His son, Sir John, M.P., received a Baronetcy 1665.

The tartan here shown was approved as correct by the late Sir Ian Malcolm of Poltalloch.

The general impression is that this family, having lost trace of the original sett, endeavoured to have it prepared from the recollection of aged natives of Argyllshire, but, as might be expected, the recovery of the old sett shows that marked deviations had been made.

40 MACCALLUM, OLD

THE CLAN MACDONALD

War Cry :—" Fraoch Eilean " (" The Heathery Isle ").
Badge :—Fraoch gorm (Common Heath).

THE clan, reckoned the oldest and most famous of Scottish
clans, descends from Donald, grandson of Somerled, King of
the Isles, in the twelfth century. The name Somerled is Norse,
Sumarlidhi—mariner. He died in 1164, and was buried in
Saddel Monastery, leaving three sons—Dugall, Reginald, and
Angus.

The southern Isles and a portion of Argyll were thus divided
among the sons of Somerled : Lorn, Mull, and Jura to Dugall ;
Kintyre and Islay to Reginald ; Bute, with part of Arran and the
roughbounds, from Ardnamurchan to Glenelg, to Angus.

Reginald was succeeded by his son, Donald of Isla, from
whom the Clan Donald takes its name. His son, *Angus Mor*,
Lord of the Isles, was succeeded by Alexander, his eldest son,
who with his issue were banished for opposing the Bruce. The
next brother, *Angus Og*, Lord of the Isles, was father of " Good
John of Isla," who settled the succession on the son of his
second marriage with Princess Margaret, viz., Donald, Lord of
the Isles, who fought Harlaw 1411, and gained the Earldom of
Ross. His son, Alexander, Earl of Ross, Lord of the Isles and
Chief of Macdonald, had three sons : (1) John, Lord of the
Isles, who resigned his honours to the King 1494, and whose
grandson, Angus, expired after a treasonable treaty with England
1545 ; (2) Celestine of Lochalsh, in favour of whose heir-of line,
Angus Macdonell of Glengarry, the Chiefship was restored,
with the title Lord Macdonell and Aros, 1660, to " heirsmale of
his body," which lapsed 1680 ; (3) Hugh of Sleate, in favour of
whose descendant the Name and Representation of Macdonald
was restored by erection of the Barony of Macdonald 1727. His
son was created Lord Macdonald, 1776, whose great-grandson,
Ronald, 6th Lord, and Baron of Macdonald, Chief of Macdonald
(and 22nd Chief of Sleate until 1910, when the Sleate Baronetcy
and representation was adjudged to his cousin), remained as
" inheritor of the Macdonald estate," Chief of the Name. He
was in 1947 succeeded by his grandson, Alexander Macdonald of
Macdonald, 7th Lord Macdonald, who, as Baron of Macdonald,
revested in the ancient undifferenced arms of Macdonald, was
The Macdonald of Macdonald, hereditary Chief of the Macdonalds. He was succeeded in the chiefship in 1970 by his son
Godfrey, 8th Lord Macdonald. His seats are Armadale and
Dunscaith Castle in Skye.

41 MACDONALD

MACDONALD OF CLANRANALD

War Cry :—" Dh' aindeòin co theireadh e "
(Gainsay who dare).
Badge :—Fraoch gorm (Common Heath).

THE name and descent of this clan are derived from Ranald, son of John, 7th Lord of the Isles, by his first wife, Amie MacRuari *de Insulis*. Although this marriage was set aside by Papal authority preparatory to Lord John's second marriage with Princess Margaret, Ranald duly succeeded to Castle Tirrim and the vast estates of his mother.

Dougall, Chief of Clanranald in the sixteenth century, made himself so hated by his cruelty that his clansmen slew him. Command of the clan and lands was then given to Alistair Alanson, his uncle, to the exclusion of Dougall's son. Alistair died in 1530. John of Moydart, his son by a handfast marriage, was " legitimated " in 1531 by the Crown, and invested in the family stronghold as Chief of Clanranald. On account of his turbulence, however, he was imprisoned by James V. Ranald (a son of Alan MacRuaridh, Chief of Clanranald, 1481–1509), who was called Gallda, *i.e.* " the Stranger," because he had been fostered with the Frasers, endeavoured with the assistance of Lord Lovat to reduce the rights which John Moydertach had obtained, but was killed at the battle of Blarnaleine in 1544. MacDonald of Morar became heir-male and of law, but Ian Moydertach retained the chiefship under tanistry and Crown recognition and lived until 1584.

His son, Alan, who married a daughter of MacLeod of Harris, died in 1593 ; while Alan's son, Sir Donald, who was knighted by James VI., died in 1619. John of Clanranald, the son of Sir Donald, served in 1644 in the Wars of Montrose, and died in old age at Uist in 1670. He was succeeded by his son, Donald (who was registered as Captain of Clanranald in Lyon Register, 1672). Donald died in 1686. His son, Alan, led the right wing of the Jacobite army at Sheriffmuir, where he fell.

Ranald, Chief in 1745, was " out " with the Prince—with 700 men. He lived in exile after Culloden. Angus R. MacDonald, 23rd of Clanranald, died without issue 1944. The Chiefship, claimed by Boisdale and Waternish, was by Lyon Court 1956 decided to be in the former, Ranald Alexander MacDonald of Clanranald becoming 25th Chief.

The patronymic *Mac Mhic Ailein* originated with Ian Moydertach, who was not legally chief until 1531.

42 MACDONALD OF CLANRANALD

THE MACDONALDS OF SLEAT

Badge :—Fraoch gorm (Common Heath).

THE Macdonalds of Sleat are descended from Hugh, son of a handfast marriage of Alexander, Earl of Ross, and Lord of the Isles—hence their patronymic of *Clann Uisdein*, or Children of Hugh. This seat connected with the Barony of Sleat was the fortalice of Dunskaith, south of Sleat.

Hugh, 1st Chief, died in 1498, and was succeeded by his son, (by Finvola M'Ian of Ardnamurchan), who died without issue in 1502. His half-brother, Donald Gallach (so styled because his mother was Elizabeth Gunn, daughter of the Coroner of Caithness) obtained possession of Sleat, but was murdered by a half-brother in 1506. His son, Donald Grumach, died in 1534, and was succeeded by his elder son, Donald Gorm, who claimed the Lordship of the Isles, and was killed in 1539 at his siege of Eileandonan Castle in pursuit of his claim. He was succeeded by his son, Donald, known as *Dòmhnull Gorm Sasunnach*, on account of his having spent part of his minority in England. He died in 1585, and was succeeded by Donald Gorm Mór, his son. Donald Gorm Mór died without issue, and was succeeded by his nephew, Sir Donald Macdonald of Sleat, 1st Baronet, created 1625 with special provision that its precedence be second in the order of Baronets of Nova Scotia. In 1727 the Sleat and other estates were united into a Barony of Macdonald for Alexander, then Chief of the Name, but the Baronetcy continued " of Sleat."

Sir Alexander, 9th Baronet, was in 1776 created Lord Macdonald. Godfrey, 3rd Lord, having inherited Bosville of Thorpe's Yorkshire estate, settled this on his first-born son who took the name *Bosville*, which was kept for 78 years, and ceasing to be " Macdonald " became head of the Bosville family. Meanwhile the Macdonald estates and Chiefship descended with the Lordship of Macdonald to Ronald, 6th Lord, Chief of Macdonald, and 21st of Sleat, until 1910, when Sir Alexander Bosville-Macdonald (resuming the name and Sleat Baronetcy) was recognised by Lyon Court as 22nd of Sleat, 14th Bt. His descendant Sir Ian Bosville-Macdonald 17th Bt. is now 25th Chief of Sleat under the judgment of 1910. His seat is Thorpe in Yorkshire.

43 MACDONALD OF SLEAT, DRESS

THE MACDONELLS OF GLENGARRY

War Cry :—" Creagan-an-fhithich "
(" The Raven's Rock ").
Badge :—Fraoch gorm (Common Heath).

JOHN, 7th Lord of the Isles, granted to Reginald, his second son by Amie MacRuari, a charter of many lands, including lands in Lochaber. The family had also lands in North Morar, and this was probably the first land they possessed, for the early representatives of the family are on record as " of Morar and Glengarry."

Alexander, the son of Donald, is referred to in several MS. histories as the first of the MacDonell family who possessed Glengarry ; but the earliest recorded evidence of the actual possession of a MacDonell of the Clanranald branch of the lands of Glengarry is no further back than the year 1496. It is more than probable, however, that for a hundred years prior to this date the family, through a succession of chieftains, occupied the lands of Glengarry.

Alistair, 6th of Glengarry, who had a charter of Castle-Strome in 1519, married Margaret, daughter and heiress of Sir Alexander Macdonald of Lochalsh—a grandson of Celestine of Lochalsh, a son of the 9th Lord of the Isles. Glengarry was erected into a feudal barony in 1574, and in 1660 Angus, 9th of Glengarry, was created a peer as Lord MacDonell and Aros and recognised as Chief of the Clan by the Privy Council 1672. This peerage, however, expired in his line at his death, when the representation of *Macdonald of Macdonald* was re-created in the House of Sleate, whilst Lord MacDonell was succeeded in the representation of *Glengarry* by his cousin Ranald (second of Scotus) as 10th of Glengarry.

In " the '45 " the MacDonells of Glengarry took an active part, being present at Falkirk and Culloden. After Culloden, Old Glengarry was taken prisoner and immured in Edinburgh Castle.

Alister Ronaldson MacDonell of Glengarry may be called the last representative of the Highland Chief of history. He wore the Highland dress on all occasions, and was invariably accompanied by a body of retainers in full Highland costume. He was accidentally drowned in 1828. Soon after, the estate, excepting the ruined castle, was sold. The present head of this ancient house is Æneas Ranald Donald MacDonell of Glengarry, 22nd and present Chief of Glengarry.

44 MACDONELL OF GLENGARRY

THE MACDONELLS OF KEPPOCH

War Cry :—" Dia is Naomh Aindrea " (" God and
St. Andrew ").
Badge :—Fraoch Geal (White Heather).

WHEN Angus Og's son, John, Lord of the Isles, came to ap-
portion his estates between the children of his two marriages,
according to the marriage settlement made with his second
father-in-law, Robert II., the Lordship of Lochaber was given
to the third and youngest son of the second marriage, *Alastair
Carrach*, the first MacDonell of Keppoch and Garragach. He
took an active part in supporting the claims of his brother,
Donald, Lord of the Isles, to the Earldom of Ross, with the
result that, on the death of Lord Donald in 1425, the Lordship
of Lochaber was forfeited to the Crown, by whom it was bestowed
on a natural son of the Earl of Mar. This grant was afterwards
cancelled, but the Lordship of Lochaber reverted not to Alastair
Carrach, but to the Lord of the Isles, by whom the lands of
Lochaber were subsequently granted to the Mackintosh Chief,
an arrangement afterwards confirmed by the Crown. The
superiority, however, remained with the Lord of the Isles, who
restored it to Alastair Carrach. The latter arrangement was
never confirmed by the Crown, and, on the final forfeiture of the
Lordship of the Isles in 1493, Angus, 2nd MacDonell of Keppoch,
had to maintain his position in Lochaber by his strong right
hand. This he and his successors succeeded in doing for two
and a half centuries. Not until the final downfall of the clan
system, immediately after the battle of Culloden (1746), did
Mackintosh become the real Lord, and the erstwhile Lords, the
brave Keppochs, had to yield perforce to the law, recognising
that the day of the sword was gone.

The patronymic *Mac-Mhic Raonuill* was derived from Ronald
Mor (VII.) of Keppoch ; while the Gaelic designation of the
family is *Clann Mhic Raonuill na Ceapach*. The Miss Alice
Claire MacDonell of Keppoch became the Chieftainess of
Keppoch, and Hereditary Bardess of Clan Donald.

The sett of tartan illustrated is stated to have been copied
from a plaid given by Keppoch to Prince Charlie. There is,
however, another sett for which the same claim is made (see
Johnston's *Scottish Tartans*.)

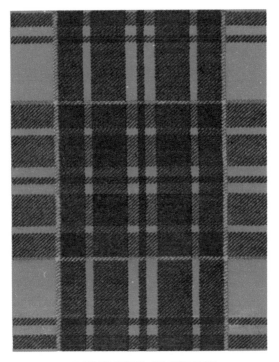

45 MACDONELL OF KEPPOCH

THE CLAN MACDOUGALL

Badge :—Fraoch dearg (Bell Heath) ; also Cypress.

FROM Dugall, the eldest son of Somerled of the Isles, is descended this clan. Dugall's mother was Raghnild, sister of Godfred of Man and the Isles. Dugall's son was Duncan of Argyll or Ergadia or Lorn. From his father, Duncan got the cradle of the clan—Lorn—and we have " Duncan of Argyll " on record as early as 1244. Duncan's son was King Ewin of Argyll, who refused to join Haco in 1263. King Ewin's son was Alexander of Lorn, who died about 1310. He was succeeded by his son, John, the obstinate opponent of Robert The Bruce, who gained possession of the " Brooch of Lorn." John was seized in 1318 and imprisoned in Dumbarton for his opposition to Bruce. He was set at liberty on the death of Bruce, and all his property restored to him.

John was succeeded by his son, John, about 1354. John's daughter, Jonete, was his heir, and in 1358 she conveyed Lorn to Sir Robert Steward of Innermeath, and so we read of " John Steward, Lord of Lorn," in 1394. In 1457 John Stewart, Lord of Lorn, granted to John MacAlan, called " McCowie " (MacDougall), and to John Keir his son, twenty-nine merklands of Kerraray, six merks of Dunolly.

John MacAlan's descendants held the lands of Dunolly undisturbed till 1715, when they were forfeited on account of the then Chief, Iain Ciar, having been present, with 200 of his clansmen at Sheriffmuir. Iain Ciar died about the middle of the eighteenth century, and was succeeded by his son, Alexander, who was succeeded by his son, Patrick, who was succeeded by his son, John, afterwards Sir John MacDougall, Admiral, K.C.B. The Admiral died in 1864, and was succeeded by his son, Alexander, a Captain in the army. He was succeeded by his brothers, Lieut.-Col. Charles Allan and Henry Robert Mac-Dougall of MacDougall, who was succeeded by his son, Alexander James MacDougall of MacDougall, C.M.G. His daughter, the present Chief, Madam Coline MacDougall of MacDougall, has her seat at Dunollie near Oban.

There is a Clan MacDougall Society in Lorn, with branches in Edinburgh and Glasgow.

46 MACDOUGALL

MACDUFF AND DUFF

Badge :—Bosca (Boxwood) or Lus nan cnàimhseag
(Red Whortleberry).

MACDUFF is the patronymic of the Celtic Earls of Fife. Constantine was Earl of Fife in the early days of David's reign, and dying about 1129, was succeeded by Gillimichel Mak-duf, also " Son of Duff " or Dufagan, probably his brother. The origin of these three Earls is unknown, but certain genealogies given for King Lulach and King Macbeth are headed " Genealogy of Clan Duff."

Certain privileges pertaining to Clan Duff are referred to in an Act of 1384. These were : First, that the Earl of Fife should seat the king in his Royal chair on his coronation day ; second, that they should lead the vanguard in every Royal battle; and third, a remission to all within 9 degrees of MacDuff for homicide on a fixed payment, with sanctuary at Cross MacDuff, which stood to the north of Newburgh. This was the celebrated " Law Clan Makduff."

Gillimichel MacDuff was succeeded by his son, Duncan, and he again by his son, Duncan, 5th Earl. Duncan's son, Malcolm, was succeeded by his nephew, Malcolm, who left two sons—his successor, Colban, and MacDuff—Christian name not given—the primary cause of John Baliol's rebellion against Edward I. Duncan, 11th Earl, died about 1353, leaving an only daughter, and as she left no issue, representation of the line of the Celtic Earls of Fife passed by official recognition of Lyon Court to the House of Wemyss.

The Duffs of Banffshire claim descent from the Earls of Fife. Possibly David Duff of Muldavit (1401), was a descendant of the Earls of Fife, as was claimed, though more likely an old Banffshire stock. His descendant was William Duff, Lord Braco (1725), created in 1759 Viscount MacDuff and Earl of Fife. Alexander, 6th Earl, was created Duke of Fife, 1889. He married the Princess Royal, daughter of Edward VII.

47 MACDUFF, DRESS

THE CLAN MACEWEN

THIS clan was of considerable importance at one time. Its habitat was in Cowal. The MacEwens were known as *Clann Eóghain na h-Oitrich*—the MacEwens of Otter—and as late as 1750 there stood on a rocky point on the coast of Lochfyne, about a mile below the church at Kilfinnan, the vestige of a building called *Caisteal Mhic Eóghain*—MacEwen's Castle. The MacEwens were closely allied to the MacLachlans and the MacNeills. In the twelfth century the Lamonts, the MacLachlans, and the MacEwens were in possession of the greater part of Cowal.

The earliest Chief of whom we have any record flourished about the thirteenth century. He was succeeded by Severan (II.) of Otter. About 1315 Gillespie (V.) of Otter assumed the chiefship. From this date there were four Chiefs—Ewen (VI.), John (VII.), Walter (VIII.), and Swene (IX.), the last of the Otter Chiefs.

In 1431–32 this Swene granted a charter of certain lands of Otter to Duncan, son of Alexander Campbell. In 1432 he resigned the Barony of Otter to James I., but received it anew from the King, with remainder to Celestine Campbell, son and heir of Duncan Campbell of Lochow. After Swene's death, King James in 1493 confirmed the grant to Archibald, Earl of Argyll, as heir to his father, Colin. In 1575 another Archibald Campbell appears in a charter as " of Otter," and in the Act of 1587 a Campbell is entered as " the Laird of Otter."

After the middle of the fifteenth century the Barony and estates of Otter passed and gave title to a branch of the Campbells and the MacEwens became a scattered clan. As a necessity of the times some of them sought new alliances. Some appear to have followed MacLachlan of MacLachlan, and others sought protection as " men " of the Earl of Argyll. Some joined the Campbells of Craignish, while colonies were formed in the Lennox country in Dunbartonshire, and in Galloway.

The MacEwens were hereditary bards to the Campbells.

48 MACEWEN

THE CLAN MACFARLANE

War Cry :—" Loch Slòigh " (" The Loch of the Host ").
Badge :—Muileag (Cranberry), Oireag or Foighreag
(Cloudberry).

DESCENDED from the ancient Celtic Earls of Lennox, the Mac-
Farlanes occupied the land forming the western shore of Loch
Lomond from Tarbet upwards. From Loch Sloy, a small sheet
of water near the foot of Ben Voirlich, they took their war cry of
Loch Slòigh. The ancestor of the clan was Gilchrist, brother of
Maldowen, the 3rd Earl of Lennox. Gilchrist's grandson was
Bartholomew, which in Gaelic is *Parlan*, from whom the clan
are designed—the letters " Ph " in *MacPhàrlain* sounding like
F in Gaelic.

In 1373 the death of Donald, the 6th and last of the old Earls
of Lennox, without male issue, left the Chief of the Clan Mac-
Farlane the male representative of the old Lennox family. The
claim was disputed, and ultimately the Earldom of Lennox was
conferred on Sir John Stewart of Darnley, who married Elizabeth,
one of the daughters of the last Earl of Lennox of the old line.
The resistance of the MacFarlanes to the *Stewart* Earls of
Lennox would appear to have been the beginning of the end of
their destruction as a clan. That the MacFarlanes were not
entirely deprived of their territory was in consequence of the
marriage of Andrew, head of one of the cadet branches, to the
daughter of John Stewart, Earl of Lennox. By this marriage
Andrew MacFarlane obtained possession of the clan territory of
Arrochar. His son, Sir John MacFarlane, assumed in 1493 the
designation of Captain of the Clan MacFarlane, then equivalent
to " chief," and the style MacFarlane of that Ilk was in 1672
officially recognised ; and in the eighteenth century, Walter
MacFarlane of that Ilk got the armorial insignia of the Chief
settled on his heirs-general, but since 1866 the chiefship has been
dormant, no one having claimed or obtained rematriculation of
the Chief Arms. The represener of MacFarlane of Kirkton
now seems likely to claim the Chieftainship.

49 MACFARLANE

THE MACFIES OR MACPHEES

Badge:—Darag (Oak) or Dearca fithich (Crowberry).

THE oldest form of this surname is MacDuffie (*MacDubhsithe*), and it is so written in a charter of 1463. The original home of the clan was Colonsay, of which they were in possession till about the middle of the seventeenth century. MacDuffie of Colonsay was Keeper of the Records of the Lords of the Isles.

Murroch was the name of the MacDuffie Chief in 1531. In 1609 Donald Macfie of Colonsay was one of the twelve Chiefs and gentlemen who met the Bishop of the Isles, the King's representative, at Iona, when the celebrated " Statutes of Icolmkill " were enacted. In 1615 Malcolm Macfie of Colonsay joined Sir James MacDonald of Islay after his escape from the Castle of Edinburgh, and was one of the principal leaders in his subsequent rebellions. He and eighteen others were delivered by Coll Kitto MacDonald (*Colla Ciotach*) to the Earl of Argyll, by whom he was brought before the Privy Council—for we learn that in 1623 Coll Kitto was delated for the murder of the umquhile Malcolm Macfee. Colonsay soon after passed to the house of Argyll.

When the Macphees were dispossessed of their original inheritance they became a " broken clan," lost their independence, and so were obliged to rank under more powerful clans. The greater part followed the MacDonalds of Islay, while others settled in the country of the Camerons under Lochiel, where they were distinguished for their bravery. This dependentship on the Camerons may account for the Macfie tartan's having a general colour-effect agreeable to that of Clan Cameron. The Macfies of Langhouse in Renfrewshire are now the most important territorial branch of the clan.

50 MACFIE

THE CLAN MACGILLIVRAY

War Cry :—" Dunmaglass."
Badge :—Lus nam braoileag (Red Whortleberry).

THE MacGillivrays, one of the oldest septs of Clan Chattan, are known in Gaelic as *Clann Mhic Gillebhràth*, and, according to the Croy MS. history, it is said that about the year 1268 " Gillivray, the progenitor of Clan vic Gillivray, took protection and dependence for himself and posterity of this Farquhard Mackintosh (5th of Mackintosh, who was killed in 1274, aged thirty-six)."

It is more than likely that the MacGillivrays came originally from the West Coast—probably from Mull—where we find them centuries ago, and where they are still to be found in considerable numbers. Those who came northward must have settled at Dunmaglass many centuries ago.

Duncan MacGillivray, who flourished about 1500, is regarded as *first* of Dunmaglass. In 1609, when the famous Clan Chattan Bond of Union was signed, the MacGillivray Chief was a child, and so the Bond was signed by three of the clan on his behalf.

The MacGillivrays took an active part in the Rising of 1715. The Laird and his brother, William, were Captain and Lieutenant respectively in the Clan Chattan Regiment. The clan was also " out " in " the '45," and were led at Culloden by Alexander their Chief, who fell, fighting, at a well on the battlefield, which still bears his name.

About the end of the eighteenth century the estate was very embarrassed, and the Chief (William) got a captaincy in the Gordon Regiment. He died in 1783, and was succeeded by his son, John Lachlan MacGillivray, who possessed the estate for nearly seventy years. He died in 1852 " possessed of some £40,000 of money, which was destined by will, including a year's rent to all his tenants." Competition arose as to all the estates except one, with the result that the patrimonial estates were dispersed.

The Chiefship was claimed by Dr. Angus MacGillivray, Dundee, who did not establish his right to the undifferenced arms of Dunmaglass or the name MacGillivray of MacGillivray.

51 MACGILLIVRAY

THE CLAN MACGREGOR

War Cry :—" Ard Choille " (" High Wood ").
Badge :—Giuthas (Pine Tree).

THE ancient motto of this clan—*Is rioghail mo dhream*—claims for them Royal descent. The earliest possessions of the clan were in Glenorchy, and they made their graves in a small chapel of Dysart, near Dalmally. Glenorchy was evidently held *allodially* (*i.e.* " under God ") by the MacGregor Chiefs, and, they not having got a charter, it was " granted " to Campbell of Lochawe. When in 1432 Lochawe conveyed it to his younger son Colin, opportunity was given to dispossess the race of Macgregor. The chiefship of Clan Gregor passed to the branch of Glenstrae, who were tenants of Lochawe, later of the Campbells of Glenorchy. These refused to accept as their tenants two successive MacGregor chiefs, thus left landless. The chiefs' attempts still to control and support their clansmen mostly scattered under alien landowners (with legal rights to their allegiance) while others were landless " broken men," brought them repeatedly into trouble with the Government. In 1603 a conflict took place between the Clan Gregor and the Colquhouns of Luss, who had been induced to execute a commission of " fire and sword," issued by King James VI., against the dreaded clan. The battle was fought in Glenfruin in 1603 and, although the result was a victory for the MacGregors, the authorities were so incensed that they afterwards aimed at the annihilation of the whole clan. Alexander MacGregor, the brave Chief, was executed at Edinburgh, with many of his followers, in 1604.

MacGregor of Roro, in Glenlyon, is the oldest cadet of the clan, and is mentioned in the fifteenth century. The last holding of the property was sold in 1760. MacGregor of Glengyle was an old cadet, but certainly junior to Roro. Rob Roy MacGregor, most celebrated freebooter in Scottish history, and a Jacobite, is probably the most famous member of the clan.

The name MacGregor was absolutely proscribed after Glenruin under the most severe penalties, but an Act to repeal the suppression of the name was passed in November 1774, and the title " MacGregor of MacGregor " officially recognised in Lyon Court, 1830.

The present Chief is Sir Gregor MacGregor of MacGregor and Balquhidder, 6th Baronet.

52 MACGREGOR

MACINNES (CLAN AONGHAIS)

Badge :—Holly.

THE clan Aonghais (Macinnes) is of Celtic origin, and considered amongst the original inhabitants of Ardnamurchan and Morvern, but suffered in the conquest of Argyll by Alexander II. Tradition says that, after an expedition in which the Macinneses had distinguished themselves, their chief was addressed by the Lord of the Isles : " *Mo bheannachd ort Fhir Ch'inn-Lochalainn ! Fh'ad's a bhios MacDhomnuill a stigh, cha bhi MacAonghais a muigh.*" (My blessing on you, Chieftain of Kinlochaline ! whilst Macdonald is in power, Macinnes shall be in favour.) The saying is an apt illustration of the use of the territorial title in Gaelic, as the appropriate style for a chief, or chieftain. Their last chief is said to have been murdered at Ardtornish in 1390, when the traditional tenure (whatever its nature) presumably terminated. The Macinneses appear to have been Constables of the Castle of Kinlochaline, one of the most picturesque ruins of the Western mainland, whose massive walls and battlements overhang the rocky estuary of the Gearrabhainn, and probably a Macinnes was its governer on behalf of the " Tutor of Kintail," during the siege by " young Colkitto " in 1645. If so, descendants of the race of the chief murdered in 1390 may have recovered possession as keepers of the castle, on which there are carvings of a stag hunt, and which is said to have been built by a dark-haired lady.

In the seventeenth and eighteenth centuries, the Kinlochaline branch appear to have been under the patronage of the house of Argyll, and to have supported the Covenanting and Hanoverian interests, but in 1745 one section of the clan followed Stewart of Ardsheal.

Neil *an bogha*, reputed the second son of a Constable of Kinlochaline, is said to have founded the hereditary bowmen of the Mackinnons in Skye and from their line appear to derive the Macinneses of Rickerby.

53 MACINNES, HUNTING

THE CLAN MACINTYRE

War Cry :—" Cruachan " (A mountain near Loch Awe).
Badge :—Fraoch gorm (Common Heath).

It is generally agreed that the Macintyres are an offshoot from
Clan Donald. It is a well-known fact that the Macintyres of
Glen Noe, Lochetive, occupied these lands for a period of 500 or
600 years prior to 1806. The tenure by which they held Glen
Noe from the Campbells of Glenorchy, afterwards of Breadalbane, was a payment annually in summer of a snowball and a
white fatted calf. The snowball could easily be got at the back
of Cruachan, and as they always kept a white cow or two, a
white calf was also procurable. This arrangement continued
till about the beginning of the eighteenth century, when the
tenant of Glen Noe, at the time, foolishly agreed to the payment
being commuted into money, which then became rent, and
was increased to so large a sum that the Macintyres could not
pay it and make a comfortable living, and in 1806 they were
under the necessity of parting with the home of their fathers.

There was a strong colony of Macintyres resident for many
generations at the village of Cladich, Loch Awe, where they
carried on an extensive weaving industry.

A branch of the clan were dependents of the Campbells of
Craignish, and are mentioned in 1612 as having given a bond of
manrent to Campbell of Barrichbyan.

There were Macintyres in Badenoch who were attached to the
Clan Chattan. In 1496 these Macintyres were, by William, 13th
Chief of Mackintosh, admitted as a sept of the Clan Chattan.
A family of Macintyres were hereditary pipers to Menzies of
Menzies, while another family were hereditary pipers to Mac-
Donald of Clan Ranald.

The Macintyres fought under the banner of the Stewarts of
Appin in 1745. J. G. Macintyre of Sorn, Ayrshire, now Lord
Sorn, is the principal landed member of the clan to-day.
Alastair McIntyre has now established in Lyon Court that he is
chieftain of the Camus-na-herie-branch.

54 MACINTYRE, HUNTING

THE CLAN MACKAY

War Cry :—" Bratach bhàn Mhic Aoidh " (" White
      Banner of The Mackay ").
         Badge :—Great Bulrush.

THE Clan Mackay (*MacAoidh*) claim descent from Malcolm
MacEth (or *MacAed*) Earl of Ross, a scion of the Royal House of
Moray. Their title *Clanmhic Morgain* is derived from Morgan of
Pluscarden, and they sprang from *Iye MacEth*, Chamberlain
of the Bishopric of Caithness, whose son *Iye Mor* got 12 davachs
of land in Durness from the Bishop, and the House of Tongue
in Strathnaver became the seat of the Mackay chiefs. In 1427
Angus Dhu Mackay was chief of 4000 clansmen and his second
son, Ian, was ancestor of the Aberach Mackays. In 1529 Donald
Mackay of Strathnaver had his lands erected into a barony of
Farr. His son, the next chief, Iye Dhu Mackay, lost this barony
in the turmoil of Queen Mary's reign, but it was recovered by
his son Huistean Dhu, who married Lady Jane, daughter of
Alexander, Earl of Sutherland, and claimed kinship with Clan
Forbes. His son, Sir Donald Mackay of Strathnaver, royalist
and soldier of fortune in the wars of Gustavus Adolphus, was in
1628 created a Baronet, and was also created Lord Reay with
remainder to his heirs-male bearing the name and arms of
Mackay, thus cailziing the chiefship. John, 2nd Lord, was an
ardent supporter of Charles I. His third son, General The Hon.
Aeneas Mackay, settled in Holland where his great-grandson,
Barthold, was created Baron Mackay of Ophemert, and his son,
Sir Donald James, 11th Baronet of Strathnaver, K.T., was
created Lord Reay in 1881. His cousin, Sir Aeneas Mackay,
13th Lord Reay, matriculated arms as Chief of Clan Mackay.
His son, Hugh, is now 14th Lord and Chief.

Strathnaver was sold to meet the debts of the 1st Lord Reay
in 1642, and the " Reay country " was sold to the house of
Sutherland in 1829.

Whilst the chiefs were distinguished as royalists, General
Mackay of Scourie, defeated by Viscount Dundee at Killiecrankie, was an adherent of William of Orange and subsequently
defeated the Jacobite army at the Haughs of Cromdale in 1690.

To another race of Mackays, in the South, belonged Brian
Vicar Mackay, to whom the Lord of the Isles granted the
celebrated Gaelic charter in 1408.

The Clan Mackay Society was founded in 1806 and resusci-
tated in 1888. Its headquarters are in Glasgow.

55 MACKAY

THE CLAN MACKENZIE

War Cry :—" Tulach Ard " (" The high hillock ").
Badge :—Cuileann (Holly).

THE MacKenzies were vassals (and perhaps a branch) of the Earls of Ross, their first Chief, Kenneth Mor, being traditionally descended from Gilleon of the Aird. Alexander *Ionraic*, of Kintail, 1427, is the first Chief on record. After the forfeiture of the Lord of the Isles the MacKenzies rapidly increased their influence, and acquired large estates in Ross-shire. Kenneth MacKenzie of Kintail was knighted by James VI. His son and successor was, in 1609, created Lord MacKenzie of Kintail. Colin, 2nd Lord, was created Earl of Seaforth in 1623.

Kenneth, 4th Earl, was created Marquis of Seaforth by James VII. in 1690. His son, William, 5th Earl, was attainted as a Jacobite in 1715. His grandson was re-created Earl in 1771. This Kenneth, Earl of Seaforth, died without male issue in 1784. The estates and the chiefship passed to his cousin, Colonel Thomas Frederick Humberston MacKenzie. The last Lord Seaforth died in 1815, and was succeeded by his daughter Lady Hood MacKenzie of Seaforth, who is referred to by Sir Walter Scott as " chieftainess," and got the chief arms, whilst MacKenzie of Allangrange, who claimed as heir-male only, got " Allangrange " arms, and his line expired in 1907.

There are many distinguished branches of the MacKenzies, and four Baronetcies held by members of the clan—Gairloch, 1703 ; Coul, 1673 ; Tarbat, 1628 ; and Scatwell, 1703. The character of heir-male (and accordingly principal cadet), it is understood, claimed by Scatwell, Ord, and others ; and Mackenzie of Scatwell, Bt., does appear to be heir-male of Mackenzie of Kintail. In 1745 the effective strength of the clan was estimated at 2500 men.

The seat of the Chief at Brahan Castle, in East Ross, is held by Madeleine, Mrs. Stewart-Mackenzie of Seaforth, who is the nearest in line to the house of Kintail, but bearing a hyphenated surname, the chiefship is claimed for Mackenzie of Tarbat as heir-female or Scatwell as heir-male. Which is Chief and *Caberfeidh* is not yet decided and Gairloch acts as " Commander of the clan."

56 MACKENZIE

THE CLAN MACKINLAY

THERE seems little doubt the country of this clan was in the Lennox district, where we find them yet in considerable numbers. The oldest account of them is given by Buchanan of Auchmar, 1723. He asserts that the chief sept of the Lennox Mackinlays were descended from Buchanan of Drumikill. After mentioning that the Risks are the first cadets of the Drumikill family, he says : " The second cadets of this kin are the Mackinlays, so named from a son of Drumikill called Finlay ; those lately in Blairnyle and about Balloch are of this sort, as also those in Bamachra and above the Water of Finn, in Luss parish. The Mackinlays in some other parts of these parishes are Mac-Farlanes." A member of this clan William McKinlay, became 25th President of the United States. He was assassinated in 1901.

Like so many Lennox clans, notably their far-off cousins of the Clan MacAuslane, some of the Mackinlays no doubt went over to Ireland at the time of the " plantations " in the seventeenth century. Hence come the Mackinlays and Macginlays of Ireland, and latterly of America.

It is a common mistake to regard the clan ancestor as *Fionnlagh Mor*, progenitor of the Farquharsons of Braemar. The Farquharsons as a clan are called in Gaelic *Clann Fhionnlaigh*, but the surname *MacFhionnlaigh* has never come to be used in English dress. In fact, the surname has constantly been Farquharson, and there were no Mackinlays at all in Braemar or its vicinity.

The small Clan Finlayson of Lochalsh are known in Gaelic as *Clann Fhionnlaigh*, and they, too, claim a traditional descent from the Clan Finlay of Braemar.

It is probable that the name Mackinlay embraces some of the Macleay clan. Some of the modern Mackinlays insist on accenting the " lay " of the name.

57 MACKINLAY

THE CLAN MACKINNON

War Cry :—Cuimhnich bàs Ailpein (Remember the death of
        Alpin). *Badge* :—Giuthas (Pine Tree).

THE older forms of this clan surname show it to be Fingon, for
in 1409 Lachlan MacFingon (*vir nobilis, i.e.* a gentleman),
witnessed a charter of the Lord of the Isles to Hector Maclean
of Duart. The original territory of the clan was Mull, where
they held lands under the Lords of the Isles. They had also
possessions in Strathardale, Skye, as early as 1594. The
Mackinnons were closely associated with Iona in the fifteenth
century, and John Mackinnon was the last Abbot.
    In 1503 Mackinnon of that Ilk is mentioned, among other Chiefs,
to take action against Lachlan Maclean of Duart and Lochiel,
forfeited for treason.
    Ewen, who was Chief of the clan in the sixteenth century,
received from the King a charter of the twenty merklands of
Meysness (Misnish), in Mull, and the twenty merklands of
Strathardale, in Skye.
    The clan was " out " in the year 1745, followed the Prince to
England, and fought at Culloden ; their old Chief was taken,
and, after long imprisonment, died in 1756, leaving two sons
and a daughter.
    Charles, his son, found the estates so burdened with debt that
he had to part with them, and Strathaird, the last of the clan
lands, held in unbroken succession for 450 years, passed from the
clan in 1791. Charles left an only son, John, the last of his line,
who succeeded to nothing but the chiefship. He died in 1808,
and the chiefship was ratified by the Lord Lyon in 1811 to
William Alexander MacKinnon of MacKinnon, descended from
a line of MacKinnons, who held estates in the Island of Antigua,
and springing from Daniel, younger son of Sir Lachlan Mac-
Kinnon of Strathaird, cr. Kt. Banneret on the field of Worcester
by Charles II. His great-great-grandson Alasdair N. H.
Mackinnon of Mackinnon is the present 36th Chief.
    There is a Clan Mackinnon Society in Glasgow, with a branch
in London. *Memoirs of Clan Fingon* was published in 1899.

58 MACKINNON, DRESS

THE CLAN MACKINTOSH

War Cry :—(*of The Mackintosh*) " Loch Mòigh "(Loch of
the Plain) ; (*of Clan Chattan*) " Clan Chattan."
Badge :—Lus nam braoileag (Red Whortleberry).

THE Mackintosh clan lands stretched from Petty to Lochaber ;
and in 1672 Lyon officially declared the Laird of Mackintosh
Chief of Clan Chattan through descent from the " heretrix of
the Clan Chattan," then on record. Ferquhard, 9th Chief,
abdicated 1409 ; from him descended Mackintosh of Kylachy,
but by tanistry the chiefship passed with the *duthus* to his uncle
Malcolm, 10th Chief, who fought at Harlaw 1411.

William, 15th Chief, quarrelled with Huntly, Lord-Lieutenant
of the North and the Sheriff of Inverness-shire. He was tried
by a packed jury in Aberdeen for conspiring against Huntly's
life, found guilty, and executed at Strathbogie 1550. The
estates, with compensation for the murder, were held for his
heir through the powerful influence of Moray and other relatives.

For the next two hundred years the clan was engaged in feuds
with the Gordons, the Camerons, and the MacDonells of
Keppoch. In 1678 Mackintosh got the usual " fire and sword "
commission, but it was not till 1688 that he could get his friends
and clansmen to help him. These, with a company of Regulars
under MacKenzie of Suddie, fought with the MacDonells at
Mulroy and were defeated. This was the last clan battle.
Lachlan, who was Chief from 1660, died in 1704 and was
succeeded by his son, Lachlan, who took a gallant part in " the
'15." He died, childless in 1731, and for a hundred years no son
succeeded a father among the Mackintosh Chiefs.

Angus, 22nd Chief, in " the '45 " gave a half-hearted support
to King George, while his wife, " Colonel Anne," and the clan
took the field for Prince Charlie.

Angus, 25th Chief 1827 to 1833, was succeeded by his son,
Alexander. Dying 1861, he was succeeded by his son, Alexander
Æneas, who died 1875. His brother, Alfred Donald, 28th
Mackintosh and 29th Chief of Clan Chattan died 1938, having
settled the inheritance of Mackintosh and the *duthus*, Moy Hall,
Inverness, on his junior cousin, Lachlan Donald, The Mackintosh
of Mackintosh, whom in 1947 Lyon Court adjudged 29th Chief
of Mackintosh, by *Tanistry*, whilst the heir-at-law, K. A.
Mackintosh of Mackintosh-Torcastle, Fairburn, So. Rhodesia,
was adjudged 32nd Chief of Clan Chattan. Lachlan Donald,
29th Chief of Mackintosh, was in 1957 succeeded by his son
Lachlan Ronald Duncan Mackintosh, 30th Chief of Mackintosh.

59 MACKINTOSH

THE CLAN MACLACHLAN

Badge :—Caorunn (Mountain Ash or Rowan).

THE MacLachlans are believed to have been in possession of Strathlachlan, in Argyllshire, since the eleventh century. At one time they owned extensive lands in Argyllshire, which are now reduced to the Barony of MacLachlan or Strathlachlan. Their intermarriages are given in the MS. of 1450, and are with such families as those of the Lords of the Isles, the King of Kerry, etc. In 1292 the lands of Gileskel MacLachlan were included in the Sheriffdom of Argyll or Lorn, erected in that year by King John Baliol. From Gileskel there is no difficulty in tracing the direct line down to the present day. In 1680 Archibald Mac-Lachlan of that Ilk, 15th Chief, got a charter uniting all his lands into a barony of Strathlachlan.

The MacLachlans threw in their fate with Prince Charles, and it says much for the popularity of Lachlan MacLachlan of that Ilk, the 17th Chief, that he was able to make his way with his men from the very centre of Argyll and join the Prince in the North, despite the fact that he was surrounded by Campbells and other keen partisans of the House of Hanover. MacLachlan was appointed A.D.C. to the Prince, and was killed at Culloden. The lands were seized as attainted after " the '45," but the next heir, Robert, was granted possession by judgment of the Court, 28th November 1749.

The three original tribes of Cowal are said to have been the Lamonts, the MacEwens, and the MacLachlans. The Lamonts and MacLachlans intermarried several times.

The oldest cadet of the clan are the MacLachlans of Coruanan, Lochaber, who held the position of hereditary standard-bearers to the Camerons of Lochiel.

John MacLachlan (23rd) of that Ilk, died in 1942, when the *duthus* of Strathlachlan devolved upon his eldest daughter, Marjorie MacLachlan of MacLachlan, who is now " heretrix " of Clan Lachlan and 24th Chief of the clan, to whom the arms and supporters of the Chief of MacLachlan were confirmed by Lyon Court. Her seat is Castle Lachlan, Strathlachlan, Loch Fyne.

60 MACLACHLAN

THE MACLAINES OF LOCHBUIE

Badge :—Blaeberry.

THE Lochbuie Maclaines are descended from Hector Reaganach, brother of Lachlan Lùbanach, the progenitor of the Macleans of Duart. He is said to have been the elder son ; but as succession depended on the father's nomination, this does not affect the Chiefship of Clan Maclean devolving on the House of Duart. Hector Reaganach received the lands of Lochbuie from John, 1st Lord of the Isles. According to tradition, these lands were held in possession by a chieftain named MacFadyen. Hector had several sons. Tearlach (Charles) was the progenitor of *Clan Thearlaich* of Dochgarroch, or the Macleans of the North. The second Chief of Lochbuie was Murdoch Roy, son of Hector Reaganach.

When John Og (5th) of Lochbuie died he was succeeded by his son, Murchadh Geàrr, or Short Murdoch, about 1494. His uncle, Murdoch of Scallasdale, seized the estate and tried to keep possession of it. Murdoch Geàrr fled to Ireland but soon returned, supported by a strong bodyguard. He made himself known to his nurse, who helped him to gain possession of the Castle of Lochbuie. Shortly afterwards he defeated Murdoch of Scallasdale at Grulin.

The Maclaines served with Graham of Claverhouse, Viscount Dundee, and also under Montrose with their kinsmen, the Macleans of Duart. Hector Maclaine of Lochbuie, with 300 men, on his march to join Dundee, was attacked by five troops of horse sent by the enemy to intercept him. The parties met, and, after a severe fight, Lochbuie put to flight his opponents.

Donald Maclaine of Lochbuie, born in 1816, went to Batavia, in Java, entered into business as a merchant, and amassed quite a fortune. He purchased the estate of Lochbuie from those who held it for debt, and thus, fortunately, saved it from passing out of the hands of the descendants of Hector Reaganach. From his grandson, Kenneth Douglas Lorne Maclaine of Lochbuie, the estate was seized under regrettable circumstances by an English bondholder. His grandson, Lorne Gillean Iain, is the present Chief of the Maclaines of Lochbuie, who still owns the historic tower of Lochbuie Castle.

61 MACLAINE OF LOCHBUIE

THE CLAN MACLAREN

War Cry :—" Creag an Tuirc " (" The Boar's Rock ").
   Badge :—Buaidh-chraobh na Labras (Laurel).

THERE appear to be two completely distinct tribes : (*a*) the MacLaurins of Tiree in Argyll, of whom Lord Dreghorn was found to be chief by Lyon Court, 1781—a line now dormant ; and (*b*) the Clan Labhrain in Balquhidder, Perthshire, deriving from Lawrence, hereditary Celtic Abbot of Achtoo, represented by the Maclarens of Achleskine in Balquhidder.

Maclarens signed the Ragman Roll of 1296, compelled for the time, like many other clans, to swear fealty to King Edward I., and they did so under three branches, represented by Maurice of Tiree, Conan of Balquhidder, and Laurin of Ardveche (Lochearnside).

An interesting and romantic episode in their history is their alliance—offensive and defensive, it may be called—with the Stewarts of Appin. It arose out of the love-at-first-sight attachment of the third last of the " Stewart " Lords of Lorn in the fifteenth century for the beautiful daughter of MacLaurin of Ardveche, and their subsequent marriage and legitimation of their son, Dugald, who became the founder of the famous Stewarts of Appin.

In local history the clan had their full share of clan feuds with their neighbours—the Buchanans, Campbells, and MacGregors. On one occasion, in the twelfth century, a pitched battle took place in Strathyre over an insult to a MacLaren, when they practically annihilated the Buchanans of Leny.

It is interesting to note that it was in connection with some legal proceedings anent the MacLaurins of Invernentie that Sir Walter Scott made his first acquaintance with the Highlands.

In 1957 Donald Maclaren, representer of the House of Achleskine, was by decree of Lyon Court, established to be Maclaren of Maclaren, chief of the clan. He held Creag-an-tuirc, the gathering-place of the clan.

62 MACLAREN

THE CLAN MACLEAN

War Cries :—" Beatha no Bàs " (" Life or Death ") and " Fear
eil' airson Eachainn " (" Another for Hector ").
Badges :—Dearca fithich (Crowberry), Duart, Pennycross,
Drimnin ; Cuileann (Holly) is the *duthuo*-badge of Ardgour,
Coll, Dochgarroch.

THE founder of this clan was *Gilleain-na-Tuaigh*, or Gillean of
the Battle Axe, thirteenth century. His axe is represented in
the Maclean crest.

John Dhu, Chief of the clan in 1325, had two sons, Lachlan
Lùbanach, ancestor of Maclean of Duart, and Eachann Reaganach, of Maclaine of Lochbuie. These brothers lived during
the reign of Robert II., and appear first as followers of the Lord
of Lorn ; but some dispute having arisen, they left him and
followed MacDonald, Lord of the Isles, who received them
with great favour. Lachlan married Margaret, daughter of the
Lord of the Isles, and was appointed by him his Lieutenant-
General in time of war, and the chiefs of Duart were recognised
in Parliament as " Laird of Maclean." Lachlan's son *Eachan
Ruadh nan Cath* (Red Hector of the Battles) fell at Harlaw, 1411.

The Clan Maclean acquired extensive possessions in Mull,
Tiree, Coll, Islay, Morvern, and Lochaber. Sir Lachlan Mor
Maclean of Duart fell at the battle of Traigh-Ghruinneirt, 1598.
His grandson, Sir Lachlan, 1st Bart. (created 1632) was an
eminent royalist, supporter of Charles I. His son, Sir Hector,
2nd Bart. fell gloriously under the Royal banner at Inverkeithing,
1651. Sir John, 4th Bart. fought for King James at Killiecrankie
and Sheriffmuir. The direct line of Duart failed on the death
of Sir Hector, 5th Bart., 1750, when the Baronetcy and (conform
to the arms clause in a charter of 1496) the Family Honours
devolved on Sir Allan, of Brolas, as 6th Bart. (Donald, 1st of
Brolas, had been younger brother of the 1st Bart.) The Chief of
the Clan Maclean, Colonel Sir Fitzroy Donald Maclean, 10th
Baronet, of Duart and Morvern, repurchased in 1911 Duart
Castle, which stands on the edge of a high cliff on the coast of
Mull. It is of great antiquity, and is a square tower with walls
of enormous thickness. His grandson, Lord Maclean, K.T.,
K.B.E., is now Chief.

There is a Clan Maclean Society in Glasgow.

63 MACLEAN OF DUART, DRESS

THE LOGANS OR MACLENNANS

War Cry :—" Druim nan deur " (" The Ridge of Tears ").
Badge :—Conasg (Furze).

THE traditional account of the origin of the Maclennans is as follows : In a feud between the Frasers and the Lobans (or Logans), the latter were defeated at the battle of Drumderfit, near Kessock Ferry, and their leader, a brave warrior called Gilligorm, slain. Gilligorm left a posthumous son, born among the Frasers, by whom his back was broken to prevent him from growing up strong and warlike enough to avenge the death of his father. This son was called Crotair MacGilligorm (the hump-back son of Gilligorm). He was educated at Beauly Priory, took Holy Orders, and eventually moved to the West Coast, where he founded and built two churches—one at Kilmuir in Skye, and the other in Glenelg. This was about the beginning of the thirteenth century. Crotair married, as priests in the Highlands frequently did in those days, and had, with other issue, a son, whom he called *Gille Fhinnein*, in honour of St. Finnan, and whose descendants became known as the Maclennans.

The Maclennans were at one time numerous in Kintail, in Ross-shire, and tradition has preserved the name of a renowned warrior, Donald Maclennan, who took a prominent part in the great feud between Kintail and Glengarry about 1600. The Maclennans appear to have been, on some occasions, the standard-bearers of Kintail, and at the battle of Auldearn, in 1645, a certain Roderick Maclennan and his brother, Donald, were killed while bravely defending the banner of their Chief.

Loban or Lobban, is a Morayshire name. William Lobane appears in 1564 as tenant in Drumderfit, in the Black Isle, where the family were so long tenants that the local proverb says, " As old as the Lobans of Drumderfit." A wooden effigy of Gilligorm, the clan hero (possibly that taken off his tomb?), was long preserved and venerated in the House of Drumderfit, but perished when this was burnt in 1715 after Sheriffmuir.

64 LOGAN or MACLENNAN

MACLEOD OF MACLEOD
(HOUSE OF HARRIS AND DUNVEGAN)

Badge :—Aitionn (Juniper).

LEOD, son of Olaf the Black, King of Man, acquired Dunvegan by marriage with the heiress of Macrailt, and his two sons became respectively progenitors of the Siol Tormod, or Macleods of Harris and Dunvegan, and the Siol Torquil, or Macleods of Lewis. Tormod is reckoned the elder, and his descendants subsequently took the chiefly style, Macleod of Macleod, and held the celebrated Baronial stronghold of Dunvegan. Ian, 4th Chief, who flourished in the fourteenth century, received the Fairy Flag, still preserved at Dunvegan, said to be the gift of a fairy princess to whom, by some accounts, he was married. William, 7th Chief, was killed in a feud with the Macdonalds at the "Battle of the Bloody Bay," and was succeeded by Alister Crotach, 8th Chief, who captured Duntulm Castle, acquired Trotternish, and entertained James V. at a mountain feast on Macleod's Table, 1536. Being humpbacked, he married Lochiel's tenth daughter, the other nine having refused him, and the succession eventually devolved on his third son, Tormod, 12th Chief, father of William, 13th Chief, and Sir Rory Mor, 16th Chief, who settled the feud with the Macdonalds, enlarged Dunvegan Castle, and is the most celebrated of his line. Ian Breack, 19th Chief, further embellished the castle in 1689, and there in 1773 Norman, 23rd Chief, entertained Boswell and Johnson. Much of the extensive Macleod estates have passed from the race but the (27th) Chief (who d. 1935), Sir Reginald MacLeod of MacLeod, K.C.B., sometime Under-Secretary for Scotland, and Registrar-General, held their ancient seat, Dunvegan Castle, in Skye and the Barony of Dunvegan and other lands. His elder daughter has, under the settlement of the Macleod estates, succeeded him, and has been officially recognised by the Lord Lyon as Flora, Mrs. MacLeod of MacLeod, and awarded the arms, crest, and supporters. She is the 28th Chief of the clan. The *Tanastair* is the younger son of her second daughter, John MacLeod of MacLeod, ygr.

65 MACLEOD OF HARRIS, HUNTING

MACLEOD OF LEWIS

Badge :—Red Whortleberry.

THE original progenitor of both branches of MacLeod family was Leod. He was son of Olaf, King of Man. Born early in the thirteenth century, he married the daughter of Macrailt. Armuinn. She was heiress of Dunvegan. By her he had two sons—Tormod, the ancestor of the MacLeods of Harris (MacLeod of MacLeod, Chiefs of the clan and Barons of Dunvegan) ; and Torquil, the ancestor of the MacLeods of Lewis. There have been disputes as to whether Tormod or Torquil was the elder son ; but representation depended on patriarchal nomination, and the House of Harris and Dunvegan was officially recognised as " of MacLeod " and chief of the whole Name.

The direct line of the Lewis MacLeods (Siol Torquil), in the sixteenth century came to an heiress, Margaret, who married Sir Rory MacKenzie of Cogeach, whose descendant was created Lord MacLeod and Earl of Cromartie, who retained the chief arms of the Lewis. The male representation and arms as " the first cadet " fell to MacLeod of Raasay now represented by Capt. Torquil B. MacLeod, 14th Chieftain of Raasay.

Siol Tormod, though no longer owners of the large territories of bygone days, still retain a good portion of the old clan lands. The seat of the Chief is still at Dunvegan Castle, Skye. It has been truly said that Dunvegan Castle is a fine old place, " combining the romance of the ninth with the comfort of the twentieth century." In it are preserved countless relics of the past.

The MacCrimmons, most famous of Highland pipers, were for centuries the pipers of the MacLeods. In modern times the most famous members of the clan have been the scions of the MacLeods of Morvern ; but all over the world are to be found cadets of the family—MacLeods of Gesto, of Meidle and Glendale, of Drynoch, of Talisker, of Bernera, of Hamer, of Greshornish, of Ulinish, of Dalvey, of Orbost, of Rigg, of Assynt, of Geanies, and many others.

There is a Clan MacLeod Society in Edinburgh. The tartan here shown is that which was, and again is, entitled the " Dress MacLeod."

66 MACLEOD OF LEWIS AND RAASAY, DRESS

THE CLAN MACMILLAN

Badge :—Cuileann (Holly).

THE origin of this clan is difficult to determine. It is pretty generally believed that they are of ecclesiastical origin. In the Highlands an individual member of the clan is referred to by Gaelic-speaking people as *MacMhaoilein* or *MacGillemhaoil—maol* being the Gaelic for bald or tonsured.

A branch of the clan is found at Loch Arkaig in Lochaber, at an early period. They were among the loyal followers of Lochiel. From Loch Arkaig the clan, as tradition says, were removed by Malcolm 4th. (1153–65) and placed on the Crown lands of Loch Tay in Perthshire. The estate of Lawers belonged to them. From Lawers they were driven in the fourteenth century. Some of them migrated southward to Knapdale, on the Argyllshire coast, and others to Galloway. The Knapdale branch soon attained to considerable power and influence. Their Chief was Macmillan of Knap, a person of acknowledged importance in the district. The direct line of the Knap family became extinct, and the chiefship went to Macmillan of Dunmore, an estate lying on the north side of Loch Tarbert. Duncan Macmillan of Dunmore had Arms registered in 1742, and he is described as " representative of the ancient family of Macmillan of Knap." The direct line of Dunmore expired early in the nineteenth century ; but the Chiefship was held to have been passed by Tanistry to a son of Macmillan of Laggalgarve, and in 1951 the representative of this line, General Sir Gordon Macmillan of MacMillan, K.C.B., was confirmed Chief of the Clan by decree of Lyon Court.

In some parts of Argyllshire the Macmillans are known as " *Na Belich* "—the Bells.

There is a Clan Macmillan Society in Glasgow.

67 MACMILLAN, OLD

THE CLAN MACNAB

Badge :—Roebuckberry (Stone Bramble), *Rubus Saxatilis* also
Dearca fithich (Crowberry).

THE Macnabs are called in Gaelic " *Clann-an-Aba* "—Children of the Abbot—being descended from the Abbots of Glendochart. The clan lands were situated at the side of Loch Tay,
and along the Dochart to the head of Strathfillan. Kinnel, on the
banks of the Dochart, was the Chief's seat.

The Macnabs opposed the Bruce ; consequently their lands
were forfeited, and the old line of chiefs (ancestors of the House
of Macnab of Inchewen) were denobilitated as traitors and the
clan extinguished as a community. In 1236, however, Gibert
Macnab of the Bovain branch was received into King David II's
clemency and in him the clan was restored. In 1336 he got a
charter of Bovain and from him the chiefs are enumerated.
Finlay, 12th Chief, was father of the sons who slew the Neishes
for an insult, when " the nicht was the nicht and the lads were the
lads." Of these *Iain Min*, " Smooth John of Macnab," pre-
deceased his father. He led the clan under Montrose. In 1745
John, 15th Chief, fought for the House of Hanover; but the clan
was " out " for the Stewarts under Acharn, Inchewen, and Dun-
durn. In 1788 Francis became 16th Chief. He is the subject of
Raeburn's famous portrait, " The Macnab." On his death in
1815, his nephew, Archibald, son of Dr. Robert Macnab, became
Chief. Owing to financial difficulties, Archibald (17th) was
obliged to sell his estates. He went to Canada in 1821 and
attempted to establish the clan there, but returned in 1853. He
died in France in 1860, aged eighty-three. His daughter, Sophia
Frances Macnab of Macnab, 18th Chief, died at Florence in 1894.
The chiefship was confirmed in 1955 to the house of Macnab of
Arthurstone, in Archibald Macnab of Macnab, as 22nd Chief and
the Macnab, who repurchased Kinnell. He was in 1970 succeeded by his great-nephew James Charles Macnab of Macnab,
23rd Chief.

A family of Macnabs were, for years, hereditary armourers and
jewellers to the Campbells of Loch Awe, at Kilchurn Castle.

A Clan Society has headquarters in Edinburgh.

68 MACNAB

THE CLAN MACNAUGHTEN

War Cry:—"Frechelan" (A castle on an island in Loch Awe).
Badge:—Lus Albanach (Trailing Azalea).

THE earliest authentic reference to the Clan MacNaughten is in connection with Argyll. The name is variously spelt. Macnaughten, being that of the Chief, is the correct clan-name. The name Nectan is Pictish. Their possessions extended over the upper part of Lochawe, Glenara, Glenshira, and Loch Fyne. Their principal stronghold was Frechelan Castle, Loch Awe. They possessed also the picturesque Castle of Dunderave on Loch Fyne.

Alexander III. in 1267 granted to *Gillichrist MacNachdan* the keeping of his castle of Frechelan on an island in Loch Awe, so that they should cause it to be built and repaired at the King's expense, as often as needful, and keep it safely for the King's necessity; and that as often as he should come to it, the castle, well furnished, should be delivered to him to lodge and dwell there at his pleasure. Between the years 1390 and 1406 Robert III. confirmed Maurice MacNaughtane a grant by Colin Campbell of Lochow, in heritage, of various lands in Over-Lochow.

In 1691 the MacNaughten estates were forfeited. The last of the MacNaughtens of Dundarave was John, who married about 1700 a daughter of Sir James Campbell, the last of the Campbells of Ardkinglass in the direct male line. It is said that Ardkinglass, Laban-like, deceived MacNaughten, who found himself married to the eldest daughter instead of the second. Local tradition says that the following day MacNaughten and the second daughter fled to Ireland, leaving his wife lamenting. In 1818 the Lord Lyon King of Arms accepted Edmund A. MacNaughten of Bushmills, Co. Antrim, as Chief of the clan and the representative of this line. Sir Antony MacNaughten of that Ilk and Dundarave, 10th Baronet, is the present Chief.

69 MACNAUGHTEN

CLAN MACNEIL OF BARRA

War Cry:—" Buaidh no Bàs " (" Victory or Death ").
Badge:—Dryas.

THE Chiefs of the Clan MacNeil claim descent from one of the sons of " Neil of the Nine Hostages," King of Ireland, and tradition says they settled in Barra in the eleventh century. Neil Og is said to have been present at Bannockburn (1314), and to have obtained a charter of the lands of Kintyre from Robert the Bruce. Neil Og's grandson, Roderick, was succeeded by his son, Gilleonan, who received a charter of the island of Barra and the lands of Boisdale in South Uist in 1427. He built much of the island fortress of the MacNeil chiefs—Kismull Castle, in which chiefly state was maintained; The MacNeil's dinner being proclaimed with sound of trumpet from the top of Kismull's tower. In 1688 Roderick MacNeil (15th) of Barra obtained a Crown charter of Barra, which was then erected into a Free Barony. This chief was a Jacobite " out " with Dundee and in " the 1745." His son, Roderick, " Dove of the West " (39th chief), was imprisoned for his share in " the 1745." Barra had to be parted with in 1840, when it was sold to Colonel John Gordon of Cluny, and on the death in 1863 of the chief who had to sell it, General Roderick MacNeil of Barra, the chiefship devolved on the house of Ersary. Of this line descends the 45th Chief, Robert Lister MacNeil of Barra, who was recognised as such by Lyon Court in 1915. He and his second wife recovered in 1937 a great part of the Barra estates. He was succeeded in 1970 by his son Ian Roderick MacNeil of Barra, 46th Chief. His seat, Kismull Castle, picturesquely situated on a rocky islet at Castlebay of Barra, is the fortress-home of the Chiefs.

Here great state was maintained by the Chiefs, and daily a proclamation, commencing " Hear O ye Peoples and listen O ye Nations," was made from the battlements after sound of trumpet, that " the Great MacNeil of Barra " had dined. A constable, " Gocman " (warder), and *luchd-tighe* guarded the castle day and night.

A family of MacNeills, a celebrated race of bards, were hereditary harpers to the Macleans of Duart.

70 MACNEIL OF BARRA

McNEILL OF COLONSAY

Badge:—Dryas.

THE McNeills of Gigha are regarded as the " eldest cadet " of McNeil of Barra, and their arms show them to be of descent from the Irish race.

The McNeills held Gigha from a very early period, and Torquil McNeill of Taynish and Gigha was Keeper of Castle Sween in 1449. The early devolution of the Gigha line is complicated. It was sold by Neil McNeill in 1555 to Macdonald of Isla. Neil McNeill, great-grandson of Torquil, was father of two sons, Neil, of Taynish, and John Og, ancestor of Colonsay.

Hector of the Taynish line, repurchased Gigha from Campbell of Cawdor in 1590, but early in the nineteenth century the estates were sold by Roger Hamilton McNeill of Taynish (Gigha having been sold to McNeill of Colonsay in 1780). He married Elizabeth Price, eventual heiress of the Hamiltons of Raploch. Their grandson, Daniel McNeill-Hamilton, became Laird of Raploch, and his descendants continue to bear that designation—their lands being situated in Lanarkshire.

Donald McNeill of Crear, a descendant of the above-mentioned John Og McNeill, acquired Colonsay and Oronsay from the Duke of Argyll in 1700 in exchange for Crear, etc. Alexander McNeill, 6th of Colonsay, acquired Gigha from his kinsman and sold Colonsay to his brother Duncan, the celebrated Lord Justice-General, created Lord Colonsay, 1867. On his death without issue, his estates were eventually re-united in his nephew, Major-General Sir John Carstairs McNeill of Colonsay and Oronsay, G.C.V.O., Bath King of Arms, whose brother and successor, Alexander McNeill of Colonsay, became representative of the family, but the island was sold to Lord Strathcona. He died in 1935, and his son, Alexander Carstairs McNeill, the present representative, resides in New Zealand.

The children of the McNeills of Colonsay were made repeat their genealogy backwards in Gaelic, on Sundays; perhaps a survival of the manner in which old Clan genealogies were preserved—the form noticeably similar to that declaimed at the Scots Coronation by the High Sennachie.

71 McNEILL OF COLONSAY

THE CLAN MACPHERSON

War Cry:—" Creag Dhubh " (" The Black Craig ").
Badge:—White Heather.

THIS clan is a cadet branch of the race of Clan Chattan derived from *Gillie-Chattan-Mor* (" great servant of St. Chattan," *i.e.* Bailie of Kilchattan), whose country was Glenlui and Torcastle, the Chief's seat. In 1672 the Lord Lyon determined that the Chiefship of Clan Chattan had in 1291 passed to Mackintosh, by his predecessor's marriage in 1291 to Eva, Heretrix of Clan Chattan. The line of her great-uncle, Ewan Ban, became heirs-male. He was second son of Muriach (himself a younger son of a Clan Chattan Chief), Celtic Prior of Kingussie, who married a daughter of the Thane of Cawdor, and inherited lands in Badenoch through a " Pictish "—presumably female—descent from a scion of the Mormaers of Moray. Ewan Ban MacMuriach, the first " Macpherson," was thus the founder of the Clan Macpherson which being thus established in Badenoch, is also called the " tribe of the three brothers " (this title alone shows they were not Chiefs of Clan Chattan) from Ewan's sons: Kenneth, ancestor of Cluny; Ian, from whom Pitmean; and Gillies, ancestor of Invereshie. Kenneth fought at the Battle of Invernahavon, 1370, and left Duncan, Parson of Laggan (from whom the name Macpherson, " son of the parson," was held to have been derived, and *not* from Muriach the *Prior*), whose line held " the three pleuches " of Cluny-in-Badenoch under Huntly ; and Andrew, reckoned 14th Chief, acquired the Abbey-castle of Grange in Strathisla, 1618. His son, Ewen, a great Royalist under Montrose, had Andrew (subject of a celebrated portrait), and Duncan of Cluny, on whose death the Chiefship passed to Lachlan 4th of Nuid, descended of John of Nuid, younger brother of the 14th Chief. Lachlan's son Ewan was the famous " Cluny-Macpherson," supporter of Prince Charles in 1745, whose grandson Ewen, " Old Cluny," was by Lyon Court adjudged Chief of Clan Macpherson, 1873. Three of his sons were successively chiefs. On the death of Albert (23rd Chief by *tanistry*), Cluny Castle was sold, but the " Green Banner " and " Black Chanter " were saved by the Clan Association. The chiefship devolved on Albert's nephew, Ewen George who died 1966 and his cousin Allan Macpherson of Cluny and Blairgowrie was recognised by Lyon Court as 20th Chief of Clan Macpherson. He was succeeded in 1969 by his son William Alan Macpherson of Cluny and Blairgowrie, 21st Chief.

72 MACPHERSON

THE CLAN MACQUARRIE

War Cry:—" An t-Arm Breac Dearg "
" The Army of the Checkered Red " [tartan].
Badge:—Giuthas (Pine Tree).

THE name Macquarrie comes from the Gaelic *Guaire*, which means noble. The Macquarries first appear in possession of Ulva and part of Mull, and, like the Mackinnons, " their situation forced them," says Skene, " to become dependent upon the MacDonalds."

John Macquarrie of Ulva is the first on record, dying about 1473. After the forfeiture of the Lord of the Isles they followed Maclean of Duart. When, in 1609, the Bishop of the Isles went to Iona as Commissioner for King James VI., among the chief men of the Isles who submitted themselves to him were Macquarrie of Ulva, Mackinnon of that Ilk, and ten others.

Lachlan Macquarrie (16th) of Ulva was obliged to dispose of his property, and in 1778, at the age of sixty-three, he entered the army.

When the old 74th Regiment, or Argyll Highlanders, were raised in 1777 by Colonel Campbell of Barbreck, Lachlan Macquarrie obtained a commission in it, and his name, under date 23rd December 1777, appears among the officers of this regiment, which was disbanded in 1783; and after a long life, the last of the Macquarries of Ulva died in 1818 without male issue. This Lachlan was the proprietor of Ulva at the time of the visit of Dr. Johnson and Mr. Boswell to that island in 1773. A later claimant to the chiefship held the office of Beadle in South Knapdale, and there are still claimants overseas, but no petition for the chief's Arms has yet been made to Lyon Court. Governor Macquarrie of N.S.W. was a cousin of the then chief.

73 MACQUARRIE

THE MACQUEENS

Badge:—Bocsa (Boxwood) or Lus nan cnàimhseag,
Braoileag (Red Whortleberry).

THE Macqueens are of Norse origin, from Sweyn or Swyne, rendered in Gaelic *MacCuine, MacShuibhne.* A Sween Macqueen signs the Clan Chattan Bond of 1609. Although latterly regarded as a sept of the Clan Chattan, they are more likely to be of Clan Ranald origin. In the thirteenth century a family of MacSweens held lands at Kintyre, especially Castle Sween. In Skye we find the Gaelic name *MacSuain,* taking the form MacSween, MacSwan and Swan in English.

Although originally but an offshoot of the Hebridean Macqueens who owed allegiance to the Lord of the Isles, the Macqueens of Corrybrough, who settled in Strathdearn, may be said to have occupied the position of " head of the haill name "; but Mac-Queen of Corrybrough never established his chiefly status in the Court of the Lord Lyon. One MacSween, in Grenada, became armigerous.

The Macqueens are known as Clan Revan, and the circumstances under which the Macqueens left the West Coast and settled in Strathdearn are stated to be as follows: Early in the fifteenth century Malcolm Beg Mackintosh (10th of Mackintosh) married Mora MacDonald of Moidart, and with the bride came, as was the custom, several of her kinsmen, who took up their abode near her new home. Among the followers were Revan-MacMulmor MacAngus, of whom the Clan Revan are descended, and Donald Mac-Gillandrish, of whom the Clan Andrish. Roderick Du Revan Macqueen is said to have fought under Mackintosh at the battle of Harlaw, 1411.

On the death in 1881 of John Fraser Macqueen, then regarded as Chief, but not to the estate, the succession to the chiefship, opened to his only surviving brother, Lachlan, a distinguished officer in the East India Company, who died in 1896. He was succeeded in the chiefship by his only son, Donald, now understood to be resident in New Zealand, but no steps have been taken to establish his claim to the chiefship and relative ensigns armorial.

74 MACQUEEN

THE CLAN MACRAE

War Cry:—" Sgùr Urain " (A mountain in Kintail).
Badge:—Garbhag an t-sléibhe (Fir Club Moss).

IT is generally understood that the name Macrae—Gaelic *Mac-Rath*—means " Son of Grace," and had, in all probability, an ecclesiastical origin. It occurs as a personal or Christian name in Ireland, and also in Scotland, from the fifth to the thirteenth century. It was common as a surname in Galloway, Ayrshire, and the south of Perthshire in the fifteenth and sixteenth centuries, and is still common, with various forms of spelling—M'Crae, M'Crea, M'Creath, etc. In Ireland it takes the form Magrath.

The home of the Highland Clan Macrae, sometimes called " the Wild Macraes," was Kintail, in Ross-shire, where they are said to have migrated from the Lovat country about the middle of the fourteenth century; according to well-founded tradition they were originally a Morayshire clan which migrated westward. Their tartan—from its similarity to Huntly—is probably an allusion to this origin, and the stars in the Macrae arms corroborate it. They were related to the MacKenzie Barons of Kintail, whose ablest and most loyal supporters they soon proved, and so became largely the means of raising the Barony of Kintail, afterwards the Earldom of Seaforth, to the high position it occupies in the annals of Scottish history. The Macraes were Chamberlains of Kintail for many generations, and frequently Vicars of the parish and Constables of Eilean Donan Castle. The late Constable of Eilean-Donan Castle, Lieut.-Colonel John Macrae-Gilstrap of Balliemore, restored that ancient stronghold.

Rev. Farquhar Macrae (1580–1662) was Vicar of Kintail for forty-four years. One of his sons, Rev. John Macrae of Dingwall (1614–1673), who took a prominent part in the ecclesiastical controversies of the time, was progenitor of the Macraes of Conchra, a family that has been honourably represented in the British army for several generations.

The Rev. John A. Macrae, son of the late Sir Colin Macrae, who claimed Arms as Chief before Lyon Court in 1909, was the Representer of the House of Inverinate. His seat was at Clunes, Inverness-shire.

75 MACRAE, DRESS

THE CLAN MATHESON

War Cry:—" Achadh-dà-thearnaidh "
(" Field of the Two Declivities.")
Badge:—Four petal rose.

THIS Highland clan was called in Gaelic *Mac-mhathan* or *Mac-mhagan*, Son of the Bear (*mathghamhain*)—a common name in old Gaelic times, and equally a favourite with Norse as Björn or Bjarni. The Irish form is Macmahon.

The Mathesons appear in history earlier than their neighbours of Kintail. Kermac Macmaghan assisted the Earl of Ross in 1262–63 against the Norse, especially in Skye. Their chief was one of those executed at Inverness by James I. in 1427.

All the Matheson genealogies converge in Murdoch Buidhe ten generations back (in most cases) from the beginning of the present century.

The most distinguished family of the name has been Matheson of Attadale (an estate recovered by John Matheson in Fernaig, 1738), descended from Dugall Matheson of Balmacarra, second son of Murdoch Buidhe and Chamberlain of Lochalsh. Sir Alexander, 5th of Attadale, M.P., for Inverness Burghs, was created a Baronet 1882, a title which subsists though the estates have been lost.

A strong sept of Mathesons existed in Sutherland, east of the " Cat " range, from 1492 downwards. They were no doubt a sept of the Attadale family. The chief family had its seat at Shinness. In Jacobite days Neil Matheson was head of the Shinness family. From this family descended Sir James Sutherland Matheson of the Lewis (1796–1887). Matheson of Achany is now represented by an heiress, who, although married, retains her name and designation of " Matheson of Achany " by decree of Lyon Court.

The chiefship of the clan has been stated to be in the representative of the Mathesons of Bennetsfield—viz.: Heylin F. Matheson, of Eastbourne College, whose son—Colonel Bertram Matheson—as Matheson of Matheson was awarded the arms and chiefship in Lyon Court.

76 MATHESON

THE CLAN MAXWELL

Badge:—Rowan.

THE first mention we have of the Maxwell clan is Sir John Maxwell, Chamberlain of Scotland, who died without issue in 1241. He was succeeded by his brother, who, with other children, had two sons, Herbert and John. Sir Herbert's descendant in the seventh degree was created Lord Maxwell, and had two sons—Robert, 2nd Lord, and Sir Edward. From the latter come the Maxwells of Monreith. Robert, 2nd Lord Maxwell, was succeeded by his son John, who fell at Flodden, 1513, when the title went to his son. The latter had two sons—Robert, 5th Lord, and Sir John, who became Lord Herries of Terregles. Robert, 5th Lord, was succeeded by his son, 6th Lord, who in turn was succeeded by his son John; the latter was executed for murder, and the title fell to his brother, Robert, afterwards Earl of Nithsdale. His son, Robert, dying without issue, the estates reverted to his cousin, Lord Herries, whose son and grandson held the Earldom in turn. The latter was sentenced to death as a Jacobite, but, by the aid of his wife, escaped to Rome, where he died in 1744. He left a son, William, whose great-grandson proved his claim to the Barony of Herries. He died in 1876, succeeded by his son, Marmaduke (Lord Herries). Sir John Maxwell of Pollok, great-grandson of Sir John, second son of Sir Aymer, had two sons, Sir John and Sir Robert. From the latter come the Maxwells of Cardoness, also those of Farnham. From the former come the Maxwells of Pollok, Baronets. The great Border castle of Caerlaverock was long the seat of the Maxwell Chiefs.

77 MAXWELL

THE CLAN MENZIES

War Cry:—" Geal is Dearg a suas "
" (Up with the White and Red ").
Badge:—Menzies Heath.

THE clan seems to have been settled in Atholl from an early period. The name occurs in charters during the reigns of William the Lion and Alexander II., for about that time Robert de Meyners grants a charter of Culdares, in Fortingall, to Matthew de Moncrief. Sir Robert's son, Alexander, held the lands of Weem, Aberfeldy, and Fortingall, in Atholl, Glendochart in Breadalbane, Durisdeer in Nithsdale. From Alexander's eldest son descended Sir Robert de Mengues, whose lands were erected into the Barony of Menzies in 1487. His descendant, Alexander Menzies of Menzies, was in 1665 created a Baronet. This dignity became extinct or dormant on the death of Sir Neil, 8th Bt., in 1910 when his sister, Egidia Menzies of Menzies succeeded as, and was received as, chieftainess of the Clan.

A distinguished cadet was Menzies of Pitfoddels, who branched from the stock in the fourteenth century. The family is now extinct.

In the Rising of " '45 " the Chief took no part, though the clan was " out " under Menzies of Shian.

To a Menzies Scotland is indebted for the introduction of the larch tree, which now flourishes all over the Highlands. The first larch saplings planted in Scotland were raised from Culdares, which house became (on the death of Miss Menzies of Menzies) regarded as Chief of the clan, in the person of the late William Steuart-Menzies of Culdares. His son, Ronald Menzies of Menzies, in 1957 established his right in Lyon Court to be *The Menzies of Menzies* and chief of the clan. His son David R. Menzies of Menzies is now Chief. He has gone to Australia.

There is a Clan Menzies Society in Glasgow, whose headquarters are in the old Kirk of Weem, Perthshire. Castle-Menzies in Perthshire, the old seat of the Chiefs, is a fine example of a Highland stronghold.

78 MENZIES, HUNTING

THE CLAN MORRISON

War Cry:—" Dun Eistein " (A fort in Lewis).
Badge:—Sgòd cladaich (Driftwood).

As a Highland clan the Morrisons belong to Lewis and the adjoining mainland of North-West Scotland. The Morrisons of Perth and Lennox formed no clan, and the name in Gaelic is different. The latter is from Maurice, Gaelic *Moiris*.

The Clan Morrison derive their name from an adaptation of Gaelic *MacGille-mhoire* or *M'Gilmor*, *Gille-mhoire* meaning " Devotee of St. Mary." John Morisone, " indweller " of Lewis, writing about 1680, records that the first inhabitants of Lewis were then men of three races—Mores, son of a King of Norway; Iskair MacAulay, an Irishman (Issachar or Zachary MacAulay); and MacNicol, whose only daughter married Claudius, son of Olave, King of Norway. This, it will be seen, accounts for the three original clans of Lewis—MacLeods, MacAulays, and Morrisons. The MacLeods were undoubtedly of Norse origin. The English form Morrison goes as far back as the sixteenth century.

The first recorded Morrison is Hugh or Hucheon (Gaelic, *Uisdean*), the Brieve, contemporary of practically the last MacLeod of Lewis, Roderick MacLeod, Chief from about 1532–1595. The Brieve held the hereditary office of deemster—judge or " law man," as the Norse called them. The Morrisons are still an important clan in the Hebrides and in the north-west mainland of Scotland.

Morrison of Islay, Lord Margedale, is regional chief of the Morrisons of the South West and Islay.

Morison of Bognie in Aberdeenshire, has held that estate from the early part of the seventeenth century.

Morrison of Ruchdi in N. Uist is descendant and adjudged represented of the Morrisons of Pabbay in Harris and his brother became Viscount Dunrossil.

Morrison of Ruchdi has, on petition to Lyon Court with representation of the landed men of the clan, been revested in arms as chief.

79 MORRISON
(Clan Society Tartan)

THE CLAN MUNRO

War Cry:—Caisteal Fólais 'na theine
(Castle Foulis ablaze).
Badge:—Garbhag nan Gleann (Common Club Moss).

THE surname Munro seems to be from a place-name, as the first Chiefs in the fourteenth century are called *de Munro*. In Gaelic they are called *Clann Rothaich*. The first assured Chief by charter evidence is Robert de Munro (1341-72). The clan *duthus* has uninterruptedly been Castle-Foulis in Ross-shire.

In 1544 and 1550 two bonds of Kindness and Alliance were signed between Ross of Balnagowan and Robert Munro of Foulis.

Robert, the 18th Chief, went over to Sweden with Sir Donald Mackay, first Lord Reay, in 1626, and joined the army of Gustavus Adolphus. He died in 1633, and was succeeded by his brother, Hector, who in 1634 was created by Charles I. a Baronet of Nova Scotia. On the death of Sir Hector's son and heir the direct line of the chiefs became extinct. The title and property then passed to Robert Munro of Opisdale, grandson of George, third son of the 15th Chief of Foulis.

In 1740, when the independent companies of the Black Watch were formed into the 43rd (afterwards 42nd) Regiment, Sir Robert Munro, 6th Baronet, had the honour of being appointed its Lieutenant-Colonel, John, Earl of Crawford, being the Colonel. Sir Robert's next brother, George, was one of the Captains, while his youngest brother, James, became surgeon of the regiment.

The late Chief was Sir Hector Munro of Foulis, 11th Baronet, whose daughter Eva then successor of Foulis became 32nd Lady of Foulis and Heritrix of the Clan. In 1938 she resumed her husband's name of " Gascoigne " and having thereupon been adjudged " conventionally dead " (as a " Munro ") her son, Patrick Munro of Foulis became successor to Foulis and 33rd Chief, being revested in the undifferenced arms by Lyon Court. The home of the Chief is Foulis Castle, Ross-shire.

80 MUNRO, DRESS

MURRAY OF ATHOLL

Badge:—Aitionn (Juniper) ;   other Murray Badges are
Broom and Butcher's Broom.

FRESKIN, ancestor of the great family of Murray, was, there is
every reason to believe, a Pictish noble of the old race of Moray.
He probably represented a branch which supported the Scottish
Kings, and thus supplanted the MacHeth line of *Ri Morev*, hence
assuming the province name. He obtained from David I. a
charter feudalising part of the old *duthus* of Moray and his castle
of Duffus. His grandson, William, assumed the name " De
Moravia." This William de Moravia had, besides his heir, Sir
Walter, several other sons, from one of whom is descended the
great house of Murray of Tullibardine, which has long debated
the chiefship with the families of Abercairney and Polmaise.

The great house of Tullibardine springs from Sir Malcolm
Moray of Lhanbryde, Sheriff of Perth, whose son, Sir William
Murray, acquired Tullibardine in 1284 through marriage with
Ada, daughter of Malise, Seneschal of Strathearn. Sir John
Murray, 12th feudal Baron of Tullibardine, was by James VI. in
1606 created Earl of Tullibardine, Lord Murray, Gask and Bal-
quhidder. William, 2nd Earl of Tullibardine, married Lady
Dorothea Stewart, daughter and heir-of-line of the 5th Earl of
Atholl, who died in 1594. His son, John, as heir-of-line of the
Stewart Earls of Atholl, was in 1629, by King Charles I., con-
firmed in his mother's peerage, and so became first Murray Earl
of Atholl. John, 2nd Earl, was created Marquis of Atholl, 1676,
and John, 2nd Marquis, Duke of Atholl in 1703.

The first Duke's son, William, Marquis of Tullibardine,
having, with his two brothers, been " out " in 1715, was attainted
for his share in that Rising, and did not succeed to the Dukedom
of Atholl, which passed, under a special statute, to his immediate
younger brother, James, who became the second Duke of Atholl,
and also, in right of his mother, succeeded to the Sovereignty of
the Isle of Man. The attainted Marquis of Tullibardine in 1745
unfurled Prince Charles's standard in Glenfinnan, while his
brother Lord George Murray was commander of the Prince's
forces. His son, John, eventually became the 3rd Duke of
Atholl, and John, 6th Duke, raised the Atholl Highlanders. The
8th Duke originated the Scottish National Memorial. The seat
of the Duke of Atholl is Blair Castle, Perthshire.

81 MURRAY OF ATHOLL

THE CLAN OGILVY

Badge:—Sgitheach geal (Whitehorn, Hawthorn).

THIS clan derives its origin from one Gillebride, second son of Gillechrist, Earl of Angus. Gillebride assumed the name of his property, which was the Barony of Ogilvy in the parish of Glamis, Angus, granted to him by William the Lion about 1163.

Patrick de Ogilvy figures in the Ragman Roll. He left two sons, both adherents of Robert the Bruce. Sir Patrick obtained for his services lands in Forfarshire. His descendant Sir Walter of Auchterhouse had two sons, Sir Alexander, ancestor of the House of Ogilvy of Inchmartine, and Sir Walter of Lintrathen, ancestor of the House of Airlie. Sir John, 2nd of Lintrathen, had a charter of Airlie, 1459. His son, Sir James, was in 1491 elevated to the Peerage as Lord Ogilvy of Airlie. James, 8th Lord Ogilvy, was created Earl of Airlie by Charles I. in 1639, and although not heir-male was recognised as Chief—evidently a case of the Crown exercising the determinatory prerogative of the *ardrigh* in such matter. The House of Airlie has accordingly received the Chief Arms in Lyon Register.

During all the troubles of the House of Stewart, the Ogilvys of Airlie stood loyally by the ancient monarchy. For this they suffered much. James, 2nd Earl, was in 1646 to have been executed by the Roundheads, but, the night before, escaped in his sister's clothes. Several representatives of the family were attainted, for the part they took in the Risings of 1715 and 1745. David, 6th Earl, brought 600 men to Prince Charlie's standard. In 1778 a pardon was granted to his son, Lord Ogilvy, in consideration of his extreme youth at the time of 1745—he was but twenty-one at the time ; the Earldom of Airlie was at the same time revived, and the estates to a certain extent restored. The seat of the Airlie family is Cortachy Castle, on the river South Esk.

The 13th (by reversal of the attainders) and present Earl of Airlie is David George Coke Patrick Ogilvy, whilst Ogilvy of Deskford and Findlater, in Banffshire, is represented by the Earl of Seafield.

The Hunting tartan is given in Johnston's *Scottish Tartans*.

82 OGILVY

THE ROBERTSONS
OR CLANN DONNACHAIDH

Badge:—An Raineach mhór (Bracken).

THE first Chief of this clan was *Donnachaidh Reamhar* (Duncan the Stout)—hence the designation *Clann Donnachaidh*, or Children of Duncan. This Duncan was the male descendant and representative of the ancient Celtic Earls of Atholl.

In later centuries Clann Donnachaidh and its Chiefs were noted for their intense loyalty to the Stewarts.

When the clan lands were erected into the Barony of Struan, the Chief's name was Robert, and his son took the name of Robertson, which became thereafter that of the family and clan.

In ancient days the Chiefs had castles in Rannoch and at Invervack, near Struan; later, and up to about 1860, their principal residence was Dunalastair, Castle of Alexander, magnificently situated at the foot of, and in full view of, Shiehallion, in Rannoch; other residences were Carie, Dall, and Rannoch Barracks. The burial-places are at Struan and Dunalastair.

Miss Jean Rosine Robertson in 1910 succeeded her brother, Alasdair Stewart Robertson (20th from *Donnachaidh Reamhar*), in the estate of Rannoch Barracks, at the extreme west end of Loch Rannoch, on which is some of the finest fishing in the Highlands. The Barracks was originally built for the troops stationed there after " the '45," but was afterwards converted into a residence.

The oldest cadet family of Struan were the Robertsons of Lude; others are the Robertsons of Inshes, Kindeace, Auchleeks, Kindrochit, Strathloch, Ladykirk, Faskally, Blairfettie, Killiehangy, and many other lairdships, chiefly in Atholl and the surrounding parts of Perthshire.

The Chief of the clan is styled Struan Robertson. Miss Jean Robertson of Struan was succeeded in the Chiefship by her cousin, George Duncan Robertson of Struan, in whose name the Chief arms were recorded in Lyon Court, 1936. He died in 1949, and was succeeded by his son, the present Chief and Struan-Robertson, Langton Robertson of Struan, historian at Munro College, Jamaica.

A Clan Society was formed in 1893.

83 ROBERTSON, DRESS

THE CLAN ROSE

Badge:—Ròs Màiri Fhiadhaich (Wild Rosemary).

THE family of the Chief of this clan, Rose of Kilravock, settled in the county of Nairn in the reign of David I.; but their first designation appears to have been " of Geddes," in the county of Inverness, Hugh Rose appearing as a witness to the foundation charter of the Priory of Beauly by Sir John Bisset of Lovat in 1219.

His son and successor, also Hugh, acquired the barony of Kilravock by his marriage with Mary, daughter of Sir Andrew de Bosco by Elizabeth, his wife, one of the heirs-portioners of the Aird and other estates. He was succeeded by his son, William, who married Morella, daughter of Alexander de Doun, by whom he had two sons—Andrew, the 2nd, ancestor of the Roses of Auchlossan, in Mar ; and Hugh, his successor, who, in a deed of agreement respecting the Prior of Urquhart and the Vicar of Dalcross, is styled " nobilis vir Hugo Rose, dominus de Kilravock." His son, Hugh, married Janet, daughter of Sir Robert Chisholm, Constable of the Castle of Urquhart, by whom he received a large accession of lands in Strathnairn, etc. Hugh Rose, 7th Baron of Kilravock, built the tower of the present castle in 1460.

The " Barons of Kilravock " intermarried with the first families in the North, and filled various situations of high trust and honour, many of them being Sheriffs of Ross, while the 15th Baron, though an opponent of the Union, became M.P. in the first British Parliament. The Castle is an old picturesque building, situated on the bank of the river Nairn. It is still inhabited, and contains much old armour, portraits, and family relics. There is scarcely any family whose charter chest is more amply stored with documents, not only of private importance, but of great antiquarian interest.

The seat of the Chief is still the Castle of Kilravock, which has been the residence of the Roses since 1460.

The 24th baron, Lt.-Col. Hugh Rose of Kilravock, C.M.G., died 1946, and was succeeded by his elder daughter, Anna Elizabeth Rose of Kilravock, 25th baroness, and Chief of the clan.

84 ROSE, HUNTING

THE CLAN ROSS

Badge:—Aitionn (Juniper).

This clan is known to Highlanders as *Clann Aindreas*—Sons of Andrew. It is generally believed that the progenitor of the old Earls of Ross was the eldest son of *Gilleoin na h-Airde*, the ancestor of Anrias, who, again, was the progenitor of the O'Beo- lans or Gillanders, the old Celtic Earls of Ross. The first of the O'Beolan Earls of Ross was *Fearchar Mac-an-t-Sagairt* (Son of the Priest), Hereditary Abbot of Applecross. For services rendered to Alexander II., Fearchar was knighted by the King in 1215 and by 1226 he was Earl of Ross. Since Malcolm MacEth, of the race of the Mormaors of Moray, was Earl of Ross in 1160, it appears the Earldom passed in the female line—as was the rule with Scottish dignities—to the Abbot of Applecross. The fifth Earl of Ross (William) died in 1372 leaving a daughter, Euphe- mia, Countess of Ross, married to Sir Walter Leslie (with whom the Earl quarrelled). From them descended the Leslie and Mac- donald Earls of Ross. The Name, and representation, of Ross was perpetuated in the line of the Earl's brother and nominee, Hugh Ross of Rariches, first of Balnagowan. At the beginning of the eighteenth century David Ross of Balnagowan was the last of his race in the direct line. He therefore disposed of the estate to General Charles Ross, brother of Lord Ross, of Hawkhead, a family which, however, was in nowise related to his own. Upon the death, in 1711, of David, the last Ross of Balnagowan, the lineal male representation of the O'Beolan Rosses is said to have passed to the Munro Rosses of Pitcalnie.

The estate and chief arms having been settled on, and by Lyon Court confirmed to, the heir of entail, these became chiefs; but the Lockhart-Ross line never made up title to the arms, and the last of that line, Sir Charles Ross of Balnagowan, 9th Bt., died 1942, his widow now holding Balnagowan Castle in Ross-shire. From the failure of the line interjected in 1771, and of the present line to reregister the arms, succession to the Chiefship opened to the Pitcalnie family, and to Miss Ross of Pitcalnie, to whom Lyon Court in 1903 accorded the undifferenced chiefly arms of Ross. The present Chief is her kinsman David Campbell Ross of that Ilk.

In 1745 the fighting force of the clan was 500 men.

The surname Ross is from the county name *Ross*, so named from *ros*, the Gaelic for promontory.

85 RED ROSS

THE CLAN SCOTT

War Cry:—" A Bellendaine ! "   *Badge*:—Blaeberry.

UCHTREDUS filius Scoti lived in 1130. He was father of Richard, who is said to have had two sons—Richard, ancestor of the Scotts of Buccleuch, and Sir Michael, ancestor of the Scotts of Balweary. From Richard, the eldest son, descended Sir Richard, who married the heiress of Murthockstone, and died 1320, leaving a son, Michael, father of two sons, Robert and Walter of Synton. Robert's great-grandson was Sir Walter, who had two sons—Sir David of Branxholm and Alexander of Howpaisley. Sir David had two sons: (1) David, whose great-great-grandson, Sir Walter, was created Lord Scott of Buccleuch, 1606; and (2) Robert, ancestor of the Scotts of Scottstarvit. The first Lord Scott died in 1611, and was succeeded by his son, Walter, who was created Earl of Buccleuch, 1619. On the death of Mary, daughter of Francis, second Earl, the title went to her sister, Anne, Countess of Buccleuch, who married James, Duke of Monmouth. On their marriage they were created Duke and Duchess of Buccleuch, 1673.

Sir Michael Scott of Balweary was great-grandfather of another Sir Michael, who was known as the wizard. His name is remembered with awe in many parts of Europe, and preserved in " The Lay of the Last Minstrel." Sir William Scott, 7th Baronet of Ancrum, died in 1902, when the Baronetcy became extinct (or dormant).

Bellendean, near the head of the Borthwick Water in Roxburghshire, was the gathering-place of the Clan Scott in times of war; for which purpose it was very convenient, being in the centre of the possessions of the Chiefs of this name. " A Bellendaine ! " is accordingly cited in old ballad books as their gathering word or war cry, and appears on the standard of the House of Buccleuch.

Hugh Scott 11th of Harden succeeded in 1827 to the Lordship of Polwarth, and his successor, Walter George, is 9th Lord Polwarth and 14th laird-baron of Harden, and representative of the ancient house of Scott of Sinton in virtue of a resignation by Scott of Boonraw confirmed by Lyon Court in 1700.

The present Chief of the clan is Walter Francis John, 9th Duke of Buccleuch.

86 SCOTT

THE CLAN SINCLAIR

Badge:—Conasg (Whin or Gorse).

THIS clan is of French origin, and claims descent from Wolder-nus, Count de St. Clair, in Normandy. Sir Henry St. Clair of Roslin supported the Bruce, and signed the letter affirming Scots Independence. His son was " the kind and true St. Clair " who fell in Spain beside Sir James Douglas and the Bruce's heart. Henry St. Clair, his great-grandson, became, through his mother, heir of the Norse Jarls of Orkney, was Lord High Admiral of Scotland, and discovered Greenland. His grandson, William, 3rd and last Prince of Orkney, Lord High Chancellor of Scotland founded the Collegiate Church of Roslin, 1446, and being des-cended from the ancient Earls of Caithness, was created Earl of Caithness, 1455. James III. compelled him to resign the island principality of Orkney. His son, William, 2nd Earl, fell at Flod-den; John, 3rd Earl, was killed during an insurrection in Ork-ney; George, 4th Earl, was an adherent of Mary Queen of Scots and Chancellor of the Jury which acquitted Bothwell of Darn-ley's murder. He died 1583, and had sons of whom the most celebrated was George, Sinclair of Mey, Chancellor of Caithness. The eldest, John, Master of Caithness, was starved to death by his father, but was ancestor of the 5th, 6th, and 7th Earls, and of the Sinclairs of Murchill and Rattar. Of these, Alexander, 9th Earl, Chief of the Clan in 1745, was, at his death in 1765, the last surviving peer who had sat in the Scots Parliament. On the death of the 11th Earl, Sir James Sinclair, 7th Baronet of Mey, became 12th Earl. His grandson, George, 15th Earl, died in 1889, when James Augustus Sinclair (descended from Robert, of Durran, third son of Sir William, 1st Baronet of Mey) became 16th Earl and Chief of the Clan Sinclair. His great-grandson, Malcolm, 20th Earl, is now Chief. His seat is Girnigoe Castle, Caithness. Of the many branches of the Clan, the Sinclairs of Herdmanston in 1677 became Lords Sinclair. The Baronets of Dunbeath and Ulbster are cadets of the Earls of Caithness.

Sir John, 1st Bt. of Ulbster, is celebrated as founder of the Board of Agriculture and compiler of the *Statistical Account of Scotland*. The Sinclairs of Roslin were hereditary Protectors of the craft of Masons in Scotland, and Anthony, 6th Earl, still holds Roslin Castle.

87 SINCLAIR, DRESS

THE CLAN SKENE

THE founder of the Clan Skene is understood to have been a younger son of Robertson of Struan, and the first documentary evidence of the family is when the representative of the race, John and Patrick de Skene, submitted to Edward I. The lands of Skene were evidently already the property of the House, held allodially or in some connection with the Church or Order of St. John. The Barony of Skene is situated some eight miles west of Aberdeen, and the arms are evidently those of Struan-Robertson combined with the *skenes* or durks which allude to the name of the estate whence the name is derived. Indeed the original *skene*, or tenure symbol of the barony, is still in the family charter chest. The clan is known in Gaelic as *Siol Sgeine*, or *Clann Donnachaidh Mhar*. The chief's arms are: Gules, three dirks or *skenes* supported by three wolves' heads ; Crest—an arm holding a garland; Supporters—two Highlandmen (the Lord Lyon's warrant describes the dress in some detail and is of technical importance); Motto—" *Virtutis regia merces*." At Skene House a carving of these arms is one of the earliest detailed representations of Highland dress.

In 1317 King Robert I., by charter, granted to his beloved and faithful Robert Skene the lands and loch of Skene. This was evidently the basis of the Crown tenure as a feudal fief.

The family of Skene became extinct in the direct line in 1827, when the estates of the family devolved on James, 4th Earl of Fife, nephew of the last Skene of Skene. Since the Duff heirs-of-line dropped the name and arms, the chiefship of the Skenes would now appear to be vested in the family of Skene of Hallyards in Fife, whose progenitor was Andrew Skene of Auchorie, second son of James Skene, 12th of that Ilk. Auchorie's eldest son was Sir Andrew Skene of Hallyards, Baron of Auchertule, whose lineal descendant Lt.-Col. P. G. M. Skene, is held as 8th of Pitlour and 12th of Hallyards in Fife.

88 SKENE

THE ROYAL "STEWART"

Badge:—Darag (Oak) or Cluaran (Thistle), the Scottish National
Badge: (the *crowned* thistle being the Royal Badge).

IN older works this set is termed "The Royal Tartan," as such
worn by the Pipers of such Regiments as the Royal Archers and
the Royal Scots. It is in fact the tartan of Scotland's Royal Race.
   The ancestor of the gallant and Royal race of Stewart was a
Breton noble, Alan, a cadet of the ancient Counts of Dol and
Dinan, in Brittany. Crossing to England, he was appointed
Sheriff of Shropshire by Henry I. His 3rd son, Walter Fitz-
Alan, was progenitor of the House of Stewart. Walter crossed
the Border, and received from King David I. the office of Great
Steward of Scotland, subsequently hereditary in the family.
   Walter, the 3rd Stewart, assumed as his family surname the
name of his office.
   Walter, the 6th Stewart, at the age of twenty-one led his vassals
to Bannockburn. The following year he married the Princess
Marjory Bruce, by whom he had one son, Robert, who ultimately
ascended the throne as Robert II. He left a numerous family of
sons, but there is now no single legitimate male descendant of
any of the Stewart Kings. The direct male line failed with James
V., but the succession of the House was continued through his
daughter, Mary Queen of Scots, who married Henry, Lord
Darnley, who singularly enough, was the senior male representative of the Bonkyl branch, and by this union their son, James VI.,
was thus not only the heir-male (through his father) of the High
Stewards of Scotland, but also heir-of-line (through his mother)
of the main stem. Male descendants again failed on the death of
Prince Charlie and his brother, the Cardinal of York (who left his
personal heirlooms, including the Scottish Coronation Ring and
chivalric orders *which always revert to the Sovereign*, to George
III. thus tacitly nominating him "Tanist" of the old Royal line
and heir to the Stewarts' rights to the throne). Queen Victoria
thus rightly laid down that, "as Representative of the Family of
Bonnie Prince Charlie, no one could be a greater Jacobite than
herself."

89 STEWART, ROYAL

THE DRESS STEWART (ROYAL ARISAID)

THIS tartan has been named, but on what authority it is uncertain, the " Dress Stewart," which it certainly is not, being like the red sett, the Royal tartan, and not a " Stewart " tartan at all. (The *clan* Stewart sett is the " Old Stewart.") It is an *arisaid* sett of the Royal tartan, and may have been used by our Scottish queens when, like Mary Queen of Scots, they went to " Hunting." Charles II. is said to have sometimes worn shoulder knots of a tartan similar to this. It owes its prominence as a Stewart tartan to-day to the favour of Her late Majesty, Queen Victoria.

James VI. of Scotland and I. of England left, with other children, a daughter, Elizabeth, who married Frederick V., Duke of Bavaria, Elector Palatine of the Rhine. His youngest daughter, Sophia, married in 1658 Ernest Augustus, Duke of Brunswick-Lüneburg, Elector of Hanover. The son of the Elector, George Lewis, became King of Great Britain and Ireland as George I., and died in 1727, leaving behind him a son, afterwards George II. He was succeeded by his grandson, George III., who left thirteen children, two of whom succeeded to the throne under the titles of George IV. and William IV. The fourth son of George III., Edward, Duke of Kent, married in 1818 Victoria Mary Louisa, daughter of His Serene Highness, Francis, Duke of Saxe-Coburg-Saalfeld. His daughter, Alexandrina Victoria, on the death of her uncle, William IV., ascended the throne on the 30th June 1837 as Queen Victoria. Her present Majesty, Queen Elizabeth is now the representative by " tanistry " of the Celtic kings.

Whilst H.M.'s parliamentary title to the throne is under the Act of Settlement, it is both of interest and importance that under the settlement of the heirlooms and chivalric jewels upon George III. by the Cardinal of York, our Sovereign is *also* holder of the Crown according to a Law of Tanistry which has come down from the days of the Celtic-Pictish Monarchy and under which Her Majesty is both *Chief* and *Ard-Ban-Righ*.

90 STEWART, DRESS

HUNTING STEWART

THIS tartan has long been a favourite with the people of Scotland and is regarded not so much as a Stewart tartan as a variant of the " government " sett or a general-wearing tartan. What is known as " Stewart Ancient " seems to have been, as named in shop collections, the " Clan Stewart " tartan. The red dress sett being the *Royal Tartan* of the Scottish Kings. Hunting tartans were not unusual with the more important families, the object being to have a design which would harmonise more closely with the landscape than the ordinary Dress tartan. The Stewart Kings, and, indeed all branches of the Stewarts, were keen sportsmen, devoted to hawk and hound. They had innumerable hunting forests and hunting seats, the best known being Castle Stalcaire in Appin, built by the Chief of Appin as, it is said, for the Sovereign while hunting in Lorn. Kindrochit in Mar was the old royal hunting seat in the north of Scotland where the kings lodged in the *lonquard-an-righ*, or turf house built anew each hunting season.

The first indisputable reference to Highland tartan occurs in the *Accounts of the Lord High Treasurer of Scotland* in August 1538.

" Item, in the first for ij elnis ane quarter elne variant *cullorit velvet* to be the Kingis grace ane *schort Heland coit*, price of the elne vj. lib.; summa XIIJ. lib. Xs."

" Item, for iij. elnis of *Heland Tartane* to be *hoiss* to the Kingis grace, price of the elne IIIJs. IIJd.; summa, XIIJs."

The *red* Stewart tartan appears to have been known originally as " the Royal Tartan," and has been described by H.M. King George V. as " my personal tartan." This tartan is therefore that ordinarily worn as the tartan of the Stewart clan.

The Earl of Galloway is regarded as heir-male of the House of Stewart, and as nearest in blood bearing the name of Stewart is Chief of the Stewart Clan.

There is a Stewart Society in Edinburgh.

91 STEWART, HUNTING

THE STEWARTS OF APPIN

War Cry:—" Creag an Sgairbh " (" The Cormorant's Rock ")
   on which is built Caisteal an Stalcaire (Castle Stalker).
      Badge:—Darag (Oak) or Cluaran (Thistle).

THE Stewarts of Appin form the West Highland branch of the great Royal race of Stewart, and as such, have come to form a branch clan of considerable importance. They derive from Sir James Stewart of Pierston, fourth son of Sir John Stewart of Bonkyl, second son of the 4th High Steward. Sir James of Pierston was killed at Halidon Hill 1333, and his third son, Sir Robert Stewart of Innermeath, was father of two sons, Sir John of Innermeath and Sir Robert of Durrisdeer, who became ancestor of the Stewarts of Rosyth in Fife. The elder son, Sir John Stewart of Innermeath had also inherited Durrisdeer, but exchanged it with his brother for the Lordship of Lorne. He himself had married Isobel, the younger daughter and co-heiress of John, Lord of Lorne, and their son, Robert Stewart, became Lord of Lorne and Innermeath. His elder son, another Sir John Stewart of Lorne, was murdered 1463, and by his second wife left a son, Dugald Stewart, 1st of Appin, who sought to recover the Lordship of Lorne from his uncle, Walter, Lord Innermeath, by force, but by a compromise he eventually received the lands of Appin. Duncan, 2nd of Appin, was Chamberlain of the Isles to James IV. and Allan Stewart, 3rd of Appin, established the clan by dividing his lands amongst his five sons: 1. Duncan, who became 4th of Appin. 2. John, ancestor of Strathgarry. 3. Dugald of Achnacone. 4. James of Fasnacloich. 5. Alexander of Invernahyle. This is another instance of a branch-clan being apparently established by erecting five subsidiary families—*i.e.* a great *gilfine.*
   Duncan, 7th of Appin, led his clan under Montrose at Inverlochy. Robert, 8th Chief, fought for the Chevalier at Sheriffmuir. Dugald, 9th of Appin, sold the estate in 1765, and was succeeded in the representation by his cousin, Duncan, 6th of Ardshiel and 10th of Appin, whose father, Charles, 5th of Ardshiel, had been an ardent Jacobite. No proof of the Chiefship has been made since the eighteenth century.

92 STEWART OF APPIN

THE STEWARTS OF ATHOLL

THIS tartan is not to be confused with the dark green tartan commonly known as Atholl tartan, which has been supposed to belong to no family, but to be purely a district or local tartan used by Atholl men generally, particularly Stewarts and Robertsons, who formed the bulk of the population and form the " clan " of the Murray Dukes of Atholl, but appears, however, to be an old Murray tartan. The ancient Earldom of Atholl was held by several of the Stewarts, notably Robert II., his son, Walter, and his ill-fated grandson, David, Duke of Rothesay. The title was ultimately conferred in 1457 by James II. on his half-brother, Sir John Stewart of Balveny, who, in commemoration of his successful campaign in 1475 against the Lord of the Isles, adopted the celebrated motto, " Furth Fortune and fill the fetters." John, 3rd Earl, lived magnificently in his castles of Blair and Balveny. Dorothea, eldest daughter of the 5th Earl, carried the succession to the Murrays of Tullibardine.

The Atholl Stewarts were credited with a fighting strength of 1000 men, and reputed amongst the most disaffected to the Orange and Hanoverian successions. During the reign of William of Orange " 1500 Atholl men as reputed for arms as any in the Kingdom " joined the Marquis of Tullibardine to take part with Viscount Dundee, but, on learning that Tullibardine designed to take the opposite side, they at once put themselves under the command of Stewart of Ballechin and set off to join Dundee's forces. In the subsequent battle of Killiecrankie they took a leading share. At Culloden, the Atholl men and Camerons formed the right wing, and completely routed the Hanoverian regiments opposed to them.

The tartan here shown is believed to have been the distinctive tartan of these Atholl Stewarts. It is copied from a Highland dress worn by a Stewart from Atholl during " the '45," and still in the possession of a descendant.

93 STEWART OF ATHOLL

THE CLAN SUTHERLAND

War Cry:—" Ceann na Drochaide Bige " (" The Head of the
Little Bridge "), a bridge at Dunrobin.
Badge:—Calg-bhealaidh (Butcher's Broom) or Canach
(Cotton Sedge).

THE surname Sutherland is derived from the Norse name
Sudrland—South Land—the country being south of Caithness or
Gallaibh, the Country of the Strangers. The Chiefs of the clan
are descended from Freskin, the progenitor of the Murrays.
William de Moravia, Freskin's eldest son, became the ancestor of
the Murrays; while from a younger son, Hugh, were derived the
old Earls of Sutherland. This Hugh recieved from King William
the Lion the southern portions of Caithness in 1197. The 1st
Earl of Sutherland is understood to have been Walter, who
received the Earldom in 1061. It is thought he acquired the
county by marriage.

John, 9th Earl of Sutherland, Chief of the clan, died in 1514,
leaving no issue. He was succeeded in the Earldom by his sister,
Elizabeth, who had married Adam Gordon of Aboyne, second
son of the Earl of Huntly; but, as the husband and issue of the
heiress kept the name of Gordon, it came to be questioned if they
were Sutherlands or chiefs, as they would have been had they
taken the name of Sutherland. This the 16th Earl did in 1719, by
decree of Lyon Court, and was thereafter recognised Chief of the
clan (as in the 1745 Clan Memorial). In 1766 his line again
ended in a female, the Countess Elizabeth, who married George
Granville Leveson-Gower, Viscount Trentham, afterwards
Marquis of Stafford. He was created Duke of Sutherland in
1833. The Countess Elizabeth held the Earldom for seventy-two
years and seven months, dying in 1839.

Her lineal descendant the 5th Duke of Sutherland, 23rd Earl, and
Morair Chat, George, K.T., was succeeded by his niece Eliza-
beth Millicent (24th) Countess of Sutherland and Chief of the
Name and Arms of the Clan Sutherland. Her seat is Dunrobin
Castle.

A Clan Sutherland Society was formed in Edinburgh in 1897.

94 SUTHERLAND, ANCIENT

THE CLAN URQUHART

Badge:—Lus-leth-an-t-Samhraidh
(Wallflower, Gillyflower).

THE Urquharts of Cromarty were Hereditary Sheriffs of the old County of Cromarty, much of which originally belonged to them, and whilst their genealogy has been deduced from Adam, the descent of Urquhart of Cromarty, the principal family of the clan, commences as authentic history with William Urquhart of Cromarty, Sheriff of the County under Robert The Bruce. Alexander Urquhart, 7th Sheriff of Cromarty, married Beatrix Innes of Auchintoul, and had two sons, of whom the younger, John Urquhart, founded the House of Craigfintry. Walter, the elder, was grandfather of Sir Thomas Urquhart of Cromarty, knighted by James VI. His son, Sir Thomas Urquhart of Cromarty, was the celebrated Cavalier who was one of the most quaint authors of the seventeenth century, and is world-famous as the translator of *Rabelais*, as well as many other curious works, including *The True Pedigree and Lineal Descent of the Most Ancient and Honourable Family of Urquhart since the Creation*. He was captured at Worcester, and dying unmarried about 1660 was succeeded by his brother, Sir Alexander, at whose death the representation passed to the line of Urquhart of Craigfintry, in the person of John Urquhart of Craigston, great-grandson of the celebrated Tutor of Cromarty. The direct succession of this line also expired in 1741 upon the death of his grandson Colonel James Urquhart, when the heirs-female having deserted the " name," the chiefship passed to the nearest heir-male, William Urquhart of Meldrum, lineally descended from Patrick Urquhart of Lethenty, second son of the Tutor of Cromarty, being his eldest son by Elisabeth Seton, heiress of Meldrum. He was by Lyon Court Decree 1741 adjudged chief of the name, and from him descended Major Beauchamp Colclough Urquhart of Meldrum, who died from wounds received at Atbara 1898, when the name, arms, and chiefship of Urquhart became dormant, but are now established in the heir-male of the Urquhart of Braelangwell, viz. Kenneth Trist Urquhart of that Ilk, by decree of Lyon Court. He was succeeded by Wilkins Fisk Urquhart of that Ilk.

95 URQUHART

THE CLAN WALLACE

THE Scottish Wallace is a native name meaning a Strathclyde Briton, which name arises naturally in the 13th century on the western borders—Ayrshire and Renfrew—of the old Welsh kingdom, which then marched with the coasts of these counties and Galloway. Richard Wallace of Richardston (Riccarton), 1165–73, is the founder of the race. His grandson, Adam Walays, 3rd of Riccarton, had two sons—Adam, 4th of Riccarton, Ayrshire; and Malcolm, who received the lands of Elderslie and Auchinbothie in Renfrewshire, and was the father of Scotland's great hero, Sir William Wallace of Elderslie, born 1274/6. He was captured in 1305 at Robroyston, near Glasgow, through, it is thought, treachery, tried for treason at Westminster Hall, and hanged at Smithfield, London, 23 August 1305.

The Wallaces of Craigie, Ayrshire, are descended from the said Adam Wallace, 4th of Riccarton, uncle of Sir William Wallace. His descendant, Sir John Wallace of Riccarton, married Margaret, daughter and heiress of Sir John Lindsay of Craigie. His son, Adam Wallace, was designated " of Craigie."

The second line of Wallaces of Ellerslie descend from the youngest son of the said Sir John Wallace of Riccarton, and in 1888 Captain Henry Ritchie Wallace established in Lyon Court his representation of the House of Wallace in Scotland. His son Col. Hugh Robert Wallace of Busbie and Cloncaird, was succeeded in the Chiefship by his sons Hugh, and Malcolm, last of Busbie, who died in 1948, when the chiefship passed to his cousin (nephew of Henry Ritchie Wallace), Col. Patrick F. H. Wallace of that Ilk. He was in 1970 succeeded by his son Lt. Col. Malcolm Robert Wallace of that Ilk, The Wallace, Chief of the Name.

96 WALLACE

EXAMPLES OF ARMS
AND BADGES

MACFARLANE OF THAT ILK.
(Complete Arms of a Chief.)

MACKAY.
(Cap Badge of Chief Peer.)

MACNEILL OF COLONSAY.
(Cap Badge of a
Chieftain.)

CLAN CAMERON BADGE.
(Cap Badge of a
Clansman.)

All clansmen (even Dukes' brothers) except Chieftains and those with individually matriculated crests as *heads* of houses, and all clanswomen except Chieftainesses wear the "clansman" type of badge.